POIESIS

The Language of Psychology and the Speech of the Soul

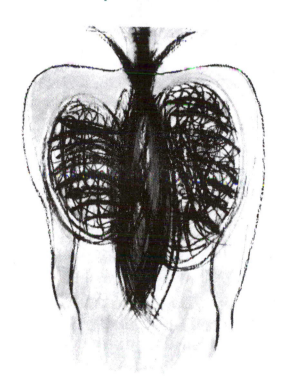

POIESIS

The Language of Psychology
and the Speech of the Soul

Stephen K. Levine

Jessica Kingsley Publishers
London and Bristol, Pennsylvania

First published in Canada in 1992 by
Palmerston Press

First published in the United Kingdom in 1997 by
Jessica Kingsley Publishers Ltd
116 Pentonville Road
London N1 9JB, England
and
1900 Frost Road, Suite 101
Bristol, PA 19007, U S A

Library of Congress Cataloging in Publication Data
A CIP catalogue record for this book
is available from the Library of Congress

British Library Cataloguing in Publication Data
A CIP catalogue record for this book is available from the British Library

ISBN 1-85302 488-0

Photography by Judy Nisenholt
Drawings by Stephen K. Levine
Printed and Bound in Great Britain by
Athenaeum Press, Gateshead, Tyne and Wear

To Ellen, Gabriel and Jesse
Family, Friends, Play-mates

Acknowledgments

My thanks to the following journals, in which most of the essays in this volume have appeared in slightly different form:

The Canadian Art Therapy Association Journal, *C.R.E.A.T.E.*, *Journal of the Creative and Expressive Arts Therapies Exchange*, *Forum für Psychotherapie*, *Mitteilungsblatt der Internationalen Gesellschaft für Kunst, Gestaltung und Therapie* and *Provincial Essays*. " 'And Yet' - Poetry after Auschwitz" will appear in the volume, *Traum, Imagination und Künstlerisches Tun: Spielräume der Seele*, edited by Hans-Helmut Decker-Voigt.

I owe a debt of gratitude to all my teachers, therapists, colleagues, students, clients and friends, too numerous to mention. My special thanks to Paolo Knill and Shaun McNiff, pioneers in the field of expressive therapy, who have encouraged and inspired me in the writing of this work. Ellen Levine has given invaluable suggestions for changes in several of the essays. Elizabeth McKim has been my poetic Muse. Many thanks to Colleen Perrin, my publisher at Palmerston Press, for her faith in me. All faults and limitations are, of course, my own.

Preface to the Second Edition

The re-issue of this book by a new publisher testifies to its continuing ability to speak to a growing number of readers. Since its initial publication by Palmerston Press in Toronto in 1992, *Poiesis* has elicited a response beyond the usual confines of scholarly writing. Perhaps this response stems from the fact that, as well as being an inquiry into the philosophical basis of the creative and expressive arts therapies, the book is an attempt to think through the historical situation of our time to find the possibility of creative living. *Poiesis* questions the meaning of suffering and asks how, in the face of human fragmentation, art making can find its therapeutic power.

As an attempt at answering this question, *Poiesis* naturally takes the form of the essay, a word whose original meaning is an attempt, a trial. The fragmentary character of the essay-form befits a thinking based on fragmentation. Indeed, the wholeness of our cultural tradition can no longer be taken for granted. In a post-Holocaust world, the European tradition has lost its foundation. we no longer know what to rely on; only memories and images remain.

In this situation, poiesis, art-making, beckons as a way of response, a path of responsibility. If we can shape the fragments of our broken world into new forms, we can find again a place of meaning and value for our lives. *Poiesis* is an affirmation of the power of art to transform life.

An attempt, however can also be a temptation, a test. Is the act of art-making an adequate response to the enormity of suffering in our time? When we gaze steadfastly into the abyss, can we still affirm the power of aesthetic response? Or are we only seeking yet another means of escape from the human condition?

The essays and poems in *Poiesis* hold both the polarities of human existence: the horror and the beauty. A faith emerges which comes not from illusion but from the ability to imagine the real. *Poiesis is always possible* – this faith stemming not from denial but from the acceptance of suffering tells us that the creative path is still open. If we can stay with the difficulty, a gift will emerge.

It is my hope that new readers will try these essays themselves. Only by experiencing one's own fragmentation can the work of re-memberance occur. Then the scattered pieces of our lives may come together and the act of poiesis bring its healing gift of beauty to the soul.

Contents

Foreword

Stephen K. Levine is one of the few contemporary expressive therapists to have the courage to develop an understanding of the multiplicity in the theoretical foundations of a domain as wide and complex as the arts and psychotherapy. Only a scholar and therapist like Levine could do this without falling into the trap of overt theoretical simplification or reductionistic pragmatism for the sake of a superficial unity. His deep roots in the philosophical tradition and thorough knowledge of more than one mode of theory and practice shine through this honest work. There are no compromises when difficulties need to be recognized.

This book acts like a kaleidoscope, projecting beauty on our screen of imagination. With each turn of the page, the fragmentation reconciles a new image, gem-like, without covering up differences. There is a strong unity in this work, even though it embraces fragmentation as an essential part of human existence. This unity, however, is inherent in the fragments, which stem from the same potential for creative existence. The reader undergoes "poiesis" even though he or she might read the chapters in a random way. In no sequence of the chapters will the outcome be accidental. It will always result in a gift eliciting meaning. Texts of such achievement can only be created by a writer who has a deep understanding and firm faith in the speech of the soul and a masterful eloquence in the language of psychology.

Whoever listens to this book may be enriched by the complexity unfolding in human existence, suffering and healing. Is it Levine's competence as an expert and actor in Commedia dell'Arte or as a poet that enables him to reach this profundity? No matter what, I always hear a message of hope: the hope in poetic imagination that enables us to express and thereby surmount our suffering.

Paolo Knill

Introduction

I was born late, an "accident", as my mother cheerfully used to remind me. Perhaps all my work since then has been an effort to show that I have a right to exist. But what kind of existence? Always I have sought the creative act, an affirmation of being, an attempt to bring something new into the world.

Can an "accident" transform itself into a "gift"? Only if there are others who receive this gift and confirm its value. I have searched for an ideal community, one in which the giftedness of its members is recognized and treasured. In teaching, political work and performance, and in my own circle of family and friends, I have sometimes found it. This book is another effort in the same direction.

With fear and trembling, without any prior legitimization from a higher authority, I offer my work to an ideal community of readers, only too aware that it may be ignored or spurned. What I wish to speak to in the reader is the ground of his or her own being, the potential for creative existence in each one of us. If he or she were to recognize themselves in my words and to feel encouraged to go on living and creating, my efforts would be successful.

The essays and poems in this book were all written for specific occasions. They retain, I hope, some of the liveliness of their origins, the sense of contact with a living audience. The danger in this type of work is that the parts will not cohere, that they will remain fragments of an unwritten whole. In a sense this is appropriate: a major theme of my thinking is the necessity of fragmentation, the refusal to find premature solutions that would only cover over differences in a facade of unity. At the same time, I find myself striving always towards integration, motivated by a hope for wholeness and reconciliation. It is this activity of working through disintegration that I consider to be at the core of the creative and therapeutic processes. I call this act "poiesis" (following Heidegger's use of the Greek word for poetry), and consider it to be at the center of human existence.

It is essential to human being to fall apart, to fragment, disintegrate, and to experience the despair that comes with lack of wholeness. To what can we turn, then, in this moment of crisis? I believe that it is at this critical moment that the possibility of creative living arises. If we can let go of our previous identities and move into the experience of the void, then the possibility arises for new forms of existence to emerge. Poiesis, the creative act, occurs as the death and re-birth of the soul. The integration and affirmation of the psyche are one and the same. But this new identity only lives in the actuality of the creative process. We are called upon constantly to re-form ourselves, to engage in what James Hillman calls "soul-making". Poiesis as soul-making; this vision is at the core of my thinking in this book.

Poiesis as integrative affirmation emerges always into form. This is the connection between soul-making and the arts, "poetry" as a generic term for artistic activity. The soul finds its form in art. That is why I have used Hillman's phrase, "the language of psychology and the speech of the soul", as a sub-title for this book. Poetry is the speech of the soul; psychology is constantly in danger of forgetting the essential connection between psyche and poiesis. In its attempt to find a scientific language to secure its insights, psychology may miss entirely the living substance of its work. Certainly we must try to reflect upon and understand the soul's speech and find a language adequate to its expression. The great psychologists have themselves been artists, shaping the materials of their own lives and work into coherent wholes that speak eloquently to us. But all too often the living texture of their thought has been lost in the abstractions of psychological discourse. It is necessary to bring poetry back into psychology, to re-connect the psyche with the poetic act that gives it value and meaning. The essays and poems in this book are an attempt to carry out this task.

Psychotherapy and the Arts

In order to understand the relationship between psychotherapy and the arts, we need to look at the context in
which therapy in its modern form emerged. Psychotherapy
is a child of the Enlightenment. Freud himself was a medical doctor and researcher whose world-view fit within the
Newtonian conception of scientific knowledge. For Freud,
the therapeutic benefits of psychoanalytic practice were secondary to the establishment of a science of the mind based
on causal principles.

Thus, during the early modern development of psychotherapy, psychological suffering was understood as "neurosis", a nervous disorder, literally, a disorder of the nervous
system.   When it became clear that many psychological
symptoms had no physiological basis, "neurosis" became a
term applied to imaginary disorders, i.e., disorders of the
imagination. The task of the medical doctor was then to
work toward the elimination of the symptom by curbing the
workings of the individual's imagination. Although Freud's
initial formulation was that "neurotics suffer from reminis-

cences", from traumatic memories, his mature theory ultimately held that neurotics suffer from the imagination, from unconscious fantasy. Psychotherapy, under the shadow of the Enlightenment conception of truth as unmediated access to objective reality, became a cure of the imagination.

At the same time that imagination was seen as the enemy of mental health, however, psychotherapy was led to give primacy to the imagination in its understanding of the workings of the mind. Freud's discovery of the unconscious as the repository of primal fantasies meant a subversion of Enlightenment conceptions of reason. Henceforth reason had to be seen as grounded in the imaginative workings of the soul. The autonomy of the ego and the objectivity of consciousness suffered a challenge from which they have never recovered.

Moreover, not only did psychotherapy reveal the power of the imagination in mental life, therapists also slowly became aware that the cure of imaginary disorders could not come from purely rational processes but only through a renovation of the imagination itself. Freud's method of free association, in its encouragement of the fantasy life of the patient, and Jung's concept of active imagination, in its facilitation of a waking state of imaginative potency, showed that a major part of psychotherapy is the healing *of* the imagination *by* the imagination.

The development of psychotherapeutic thought and practice undercuts the Englightenment assumptions from which it began. The purpose of psychotherapy today is not to eliminate the imagination from the person's apprehension of reality. Rather it is to rid the imagination of its suffering, its pathology, which takes the form of fantasies that are stereotypical, compulsive, repetitive and destructive of self and others. The therapeutic ideal would then be a freeing of the imagination, the possibility of a more creative life for the person and for the social world in which he or she lives.

Given this conception of psychotherapy and its relation to the imagination, it becomes clear why the arts need to enter into the therapeutic process and why, in recent years, different expressive arts therapies have emerged with such vigour. The arts are rooted in the practices of the imagination. In whatever form (visual art, drama, dance, music, etc.), art is always an imaginative activity, one that fashions material (paint, sound, language, the body) with a view to its innermost possibility. The artist takes the world as he or she finds it and renders it new in the light of the imagination.

Often artists have an especially acute sense of their own woundedness. They are sensitive to the pain of the world and of the soul and use their work as an attempt to heal this pain. The conflicts of everyday life and the demons of the psyche are transformed by works of art into beautiful appearance, the shining of truth. This transformative vision then can have the power to touch the soul of spectators and audiences. The latter find their own deepest needs reflected in the work.

This means that art has the capacity to heal. Even in extreme situations, people will create. The art of the Holocaust is a testimony to this ineradicable urge of the spirit. Theodor Adorno once said that there can be no poetry after Auschwitz, but in fact it is only poetry or other forms of art which can adequately express the sufferings of humanity.

The creative arts, then, can enter into psychotherapeutic work because art has an inherent capacity to heal the psyche. This fact was recognized in traditional cultures. Originally, healers were also artists; the healing process was a ritual event, and the shaman or medicine man functioned as ritual master, master of ceremonies. These healing ceremonies can be seen to recur in different forms as social life differentiated. For example, Greek tragic drama was not experienced primarily as entertainment but as a collective ritual with a cathartic or purifying effect. Similarly, religious ritual, e.g., the Catholic mass, or the Passover seder, is designed to have a healing action on the soul. It is only in the modern world-view that the healer is conceived as a detached observer working within a de-symbolized reality.

In fact, in their practice psychotherapists function more like artists than like scientists (unless we reconceive science as itself a creative process). They must, to be effective, let go of theory and be sensitive to experience in the moment. Their task is to give form to the therapeutic encounter and to thereby facilitate the freeing of the imagination in the client. Good therapists are open to metaphor and symbol; they listen with the "third ear" that hears what is not said; they see the potential for development in the person and are animated (ensouled) by these invisible possibilities.

Ultimately psychotherapy is itself an art-form. It is an activity in which a person takes the raw materials of his or her life and forms them into a significant whole. Confronting the demonic forces within, the individual is able to convert their erratic energy into a power to make his or her life anew. The self is created out of what we have been by casting forward (projecting) a vision of what we may be. The personality becomes the work of art on which both therapist and client collaborate.

Given this conception of both psychotherapy and art, it seems only proper to acknowledge the creative character of the therapeutic process and to employ the arts directly in healing work. Using non-verbal methods, the therapist can reach clients who have lost the capacity to speak in connected discourse or, alternatively, who are trapped in the web of words. Language itself, used in a creative way, can regain the symbolic potency that it has lost in everyday conversation. There is in the use of art a capacity for self-expression that is desperately needed by those who suffer intensely. The therapeutic space can become a theatre for the presentation of the self. The use of the expressive arts in psychotherapy is thus a restoration of healing to its original source: the imaginal depths of the soul. Only a person skilled in the art of "soul-making" can serve as a guide to these regions. Training in the therapeutic use of the arts is a commitment to living life at its fullest by accepting all that a person is and can be.

In light of the above reflections, some further considerations emerge. First the adjunctive role of the expressive arts therapist must be re-considered. Given the structures of power that dominate the helping professions, it makes perfect sense that arts therapists have become assistants in institutions run mainly by psychiatrists. As long as healing is conceptualized within an Enlightenment world-view, the medical doctor will be seen to have a privileged form of knowledge and thereby to occupy a special position of power. Ironically, doctors themselves can sometimes afford to be innovative in the use of the arts in therapy, since they operate without fear of being thought unprofessional. If the artistic and healing processes are really interrelated, then arts therapists will have to give up their inferiority complexes and assert their right to take an independent and central role in the helping professions.

Secondly, if the power of art to heal stems not from technique but from development of the imaginative capacity, then it makes little sense to train therapists as specialists in one artistic mode only. The division of labour in the expressive arts therapies reduces therapists to technical experts unfamiliar with the wide range of possibilities of human expression. Certainly it makes them unable to cope with the needs of different clients, some of whom may need to move or vocalize, others to paint or enact the drama of their lives. Further, there is a power in the transfer of healing from one mode to another so that, e.g., a painting becomes alive when one sings to it or performs a dance that expresses its dynamic significance. The expressive arts therapist must be at least familiar with all the major artistic modes in order to respond to the demands of the therapeutic process.

Similarly, no one psychological theory can claim to be privileged as a framework in which to understand the creative arts therapies. Often therapists find security within a particular theoretical framework; their use of the arts is then a consequence of a prior understanding of the psyche. Arts therapies are conceived in terms of more original premises as practitioners become, e.g., psychoanalytic art therapists, Jungian dance therapists, psychodramatists à la Moreno, etc. Without denigrating any of these approaches in the slightest, it is clear that they all have a significant contribution to make and that the creative arts therapist needs a broad familiarity with psychological theory in order to have the widest possible perspective within which to view himself and his or her clients. Perhaps ultimately a "theory indigenous to art" (in Shaun McNiff's words) will emerge to provide a single theoretical foundation for our work; perhaps we will always be experimental and innovative in theory as well as in practice. At any rate, it is important that there be no foreclosure of the field in terms of theoretical possibilities.

Finally, if, as we have said, art and therapy are essentially united, then it may be most proper to think of the expressive arts therapist as an artist/therapist. Artist/therapists need to be situated at the borderline of art and psychotherapy; ideally they will draw from both fields. Their intention is to heal and to create: to heal by creating. Artist/therapists have the dual task of understanding both the therapeutic and the creative processes. They must be knowledgeable in psychotherapeutic theory and practice as well as skilled in artistic activity. Their own art should remain important even as the work of helping others proceeds.

In addition, artist/therapists must have undergone and be constantly undergoing the therapeutic process within themselves. They must be familiar with their own pain and suffering and with the attempt to transform them through creative action. Working as a therapist is itself a way of refashioning the personality. Artist/therapists must be continually open to self-transformation if they are to be able to assist others in this task.

The expressive arts therapies stand at a critical juncture in their own development and in that of our culture. Given an appropriate framework of understanding, in which their historical and philosophical origins are made clear, they can emerge as a significant force for human development.

Especially at this point in our civilization, when technical accomplishments have raised the specter of the annihilation of all living beings, the healing power of art is needed. In the encounter of humanity with its historical fate, the possibility of creative transformation of the demonic forces of history must be kept open. The use of the arts as a means of healing the soul testifies to the inherent power of men and women to confront the depths of their own pain and to emerge with a sense that life is indeed worth living. In this way the expressive arts therapies can help discharge the debt to future generations which all of us owe.

The Artist as Therapist

Towards a Poetic Psychology

The recent interest in the use of the arts in psychotherapy testifies to the difficulty that modern psychiatry and psychology have had in understanding and treating mental illness. Psychological suffering has been understood in terms of a model of the mind in which reason is seen as primary. Reason is understood to be characterized by order, clarity, and coherence of thought, the capacity to see reality as it is without delusion. The opposite of reason would be a disordered mind, chaotic, obscure, subject to fantasies which prevent the person from being in touch with or being able to "test" reality.

In this conception of the mind's functioning, the imagination is seen as suspect, an enemy to clear thinking and accurate perception. Madness and psychological suffering are, then, diseases of the imagination. The cure would be a replacement of fantasy by reality, of imagination by reason. In the treatment of mental illness, therefore, it is thought to be essential to calm the patient's disordered mind, not to encourage his or her fantasy life, but to modify their behaviour to enable them to live in the world as it really is. The treatment of choice would be psychotropic medication to calm the patient and verbal counseling to eliminate his or her unrealistic fantasies.

The problem with this approach is not so much that it does not work but, rather, that where it works it produces patients who seem like shells of human beings. Devoid of affect, limited in their capacity to live life fully, they are dismissed from hospital only to live a half-life in group homes or to wander the streets, living testimonials of the limitations of modern psychiatric medicine.

Of course, as James Hillman has shown, the overly rationalistic model of modern psychiatry is itself an imaginal construction, a fantasy based on the image of a heroic ego whose task it is to conquer a resistant reality. This is the dominant fantasy of our culture, of which medical psychiatry is only a part. As long as we live in this fantasy, we will be at war with fantasy itself. We will consider imagination to be the enemy and seek to create an an-aesthetic reality harnessed to our will.

That psychiatrists and other psychotherapists are now turning to the arts for therapeutic purposes indicates that we have reached the limits of scientific psychology. It also indicates that our culture as a whole is awakening from the dream of the Enlightenment, the fantasy of a world without fantasy, controllable by reason.

In turning to the arts for healing, we are re-discovering an ancient tradition. In early societies and in indigenous cultures, all healing takes place through ceremonial means. Music, dance, song, story-telling, mask-making, the creation of visual imagery and the ritual re-enactment of myth are all components of a communal process in which suffering is given form. The healer, as shaman, medicine man, sorcerer or witch doctor, joins with the community to find the form to contain and release the suffering of the one who is ill. Often healers have suffered from the illness themselves and gained their power to heal from the knowledge of their own suffering. This archetype of the wounded healer contrasts strongly with the image of the modern doctor who is "well" treating the patient who is "ill."

Typically, shamanic healers enter a trance state, occasioned by the drum and the dance, where they experience an ecstatic release of their spirit. The spirit then journeys to the land of the gods where it may engage in mortal combat for the soul of the one who suffers. Upon returning, shamen are able to use the powers they have gained from the spirit world to heal others. Their journey is possible only within the communal structure of myth and ritual which sustain both healer and sufferer.

Shamanic healers are sustained in their journey by the ritual intimacy of the community which prepares their way and welcomes them back. The sufferer is "held" by the community while his soul undergoes treatment. The community thus serves as a bond between the healer and the one who suffers.

Shamen are the prototype of the artist as therapist. They are masters of ceremonies who employ diverse media for healing purposes. Their healing is accomplished by a journey to the other world, the world of the spirits or gods. This journey is perilous, since they may lose their own souls in the process and be unable to return. Only their inherence in the community ensures that they will have a home to return to.

In the historical development of Western culture, art and healing have been divorced. Artists have lost their place in the community and have been relegated to the role of outsiders. Their journey into the other world is perceived as an escape from their social responsibilities. Many artists have affirmed this negative identity and proudly asserted their opposition to bourgeois society. In fact, there is a basis for this view of the artist. The moment of liminality, of chaos and disorder, of ecstatic separation, is one based, as Nietzsche saw, on solitude and suffering. The artist is alone at the moment of confrontation with alien powers. These powers may be helpful or destructive. He or she may or may not be able to harness their energies. He or she may fail and lose themselves in the process.

Further, in a culture based on the denial of transcendence, artists must maintain their separate identities. Bourgeois culture has historically been inimical to art. Art-works have become property or emblems of worldly success. Artists have become pets of the rich or entrepreneurs themselves, obsessed with commercial values. It seems that in order to remain true to their vocation, artists must maintain their separateness from the cultural world around them.

But this isolation is bought at a price. Art becomes ineffective, mere entertainment, an escape or diversion from the an-aesthetic reality we have constructed. The healing power of art is lost as artists lose their connection with a living community. Healing itself becomes the property of medical or psychological specialists who see the world through a non-artistic vision.

Nietzsche called this non-artistic vision of the world an Apollonian one. He used the image of the Greek god Apollo to personify the notions of order, clarity and coherence that belong to the modern scientific concept of reason.

Apollo as the god of light, the sun-god, and as the god of justice who sanctifies the laws of the *polis* stands in sharp contrast to Dionysus, the god of the vine, of drunkenness, disorder, and communal ecstasy. For Nietzsche, Apollo represents the isolated individual in opposition to the Dionysian community. Apollonian reason is the mode of thinking of men or women who are separated from Nature, from their fellows, from their own bodies. Dionysus, on the other hand, brings people together, as those who celebrate the harvest are brought together in their drunken revels. Dionysian celebrants experience the power of *communitas* as they lose the sense of a separate self.

Nietzsche saw modern men or women as having forgotten their devotion to Dionysus. The modern individual is devoted to Apollonian clarity and light; he or she recognizes only the principles of order and autonomy. Their pure type is the scientist. By forgetting Dionysus, they have also forgotten their senses, their inherence in a community, their belongingness to the Earth. For Nietzsche, this loss of the Dionysian was a terrifying possibility, one which would ultimately one which would ultimately lead to nihilism, as the isolated thinkers of modernity would discover themselves alone in the universe, without a foundation for their thought. Then the need to control and dominate would be without limit.

As a counter-image to the domination of the scientific principle, Nietzsche looked back to the height of classical Greek culture, as expressed in Greek tragedy. The tragic drama of the Greeks, with its exquisite poetry, had been conceived by philologists before Nietzsche as an art of supreme order and harmony. Nietzsche broke this image by re-calling the ritual origins of tragic drama in the Dionysian festivals. The celebration of the tragic drama in Greece was in fact dedicated to the god Dionysus, and Nietzsche saw the tragic chorus as the continuation of the Dionysian throng. The poetry of the protagonist gains its power only on the foundation of choral song and dance. Thus one could say that the tragic drama is a unity of Apollonian words and Dionysian music.

For Nietzsche, tragedy represents the essence of an artistic culture in opposition to our scientific one. The death of tragedy is the death of vital art. By losing art, we also lose the Dionysian, the connection to all that transcends our petty little individuality, our narcissism.

Nietzsche did not advocate a purely Dionysian culture. He emphasized the Dionysian because it had been lost sight of in the scientific world-view of the Enlightenment; but the Dionysian by itself is not enough. It is power, vitality, will; but unless it is given form, it can be destructive as well as healthful. In fact, Nietzsche taught that the more the Dionysian was ignored the more potential for destruction there was. Nietzsche is sometimes thought of as a proto-

Fascist; but in a certain sense his thinking warned against Fascism well before its time.

Dionysian power, then, has to be transformed by Apollonian clarity. The result would be living form. The "chaos" of the Dionysian, joined with the "cosmos" (order) of the Apollonian, would give birth to the "dancing star" of an artistic culture. Artists must open themselves to the Dionysian forces in order to shape them into vibrant living forms. In so doing, they render a service to their entire community, communicating (in the proper sense of the word) a vision of a world grounded upon the living Earth. A community that could affirm such a world could also affirm itself and its belongingness to something greater than itself.

Nietzsche's philosophy finds many echoes in psycho-analytic theory. In particular, parallels have been drawn between the Dionysian/Apollonian distinction and Freud's conception of the id in relation to the ego. Nietzsche also has an explanation of the significance of the sense of guilt which is remarkably similar to Freud's theory of the super-ego. But Freud and his followers, with some exceptions, have remained within an Apollonian world-view. Freud never abandoned his project of a scientific psychology and held fast to the maxim that "where id was there ego shall be." At the same time he recognized the power of art and confessed his inability to comprehend it within rational cat-egories. Nietzsche, on the other hand, used imaginative categories to conceive the power of the imagination. His notions of the Apollonian and the Dionysian are imaginative personifications, not logical principles. All the concrete details of the myths adhere to them. In this sense he has formulated not only a psychology of poetry but also a poetic psychology.

Furthermore, by situating his categories historically in Greek culture, Nietzsche opens up the possibility of re-calling the ceremonial origins of art and its ancient healing tradition. The shaman in relation to the tribal community parallels the hero's relationship to the chorus. Greek trag-edy is merely one instance of the healing power of art based on its communal origins. When Oedipus suffers, the community suffers through him. He undertakes the painful journey into self-knowledge alone, but he does so for the relief of the city which is suffering from the pollution caused by the transgression of human limits, a pollution he himself is ultimately responsible for. He is both wounded and healer; and, in the end, the tragic wisdom which his suffering has brought him confers a blessing on the land. Freud was right to see the sin of Oedipus as present in all of us, but what he did not see was the healing ritual of the drama, which expiates the sin through suffering supported by the community. It is ultimately the Athenian community itself that suffers and is healed through the catharsis that Oedipus undergoes.

Nietzsche's recollection of the origins of Greek tragedy had the purpose of envisioning the re-birth of an artistic culture, one in which human suffering could be acknowledged and expressed and thereby transcended. The contemporary use of the arts in psychotherapy can be seen as a re-affirmation of this Nietzschean vision. However, this will only happen if we are able to re-conceive psychotherapy outside of the Apollonian categories of modern scientific medicine.

Psychological suffering is intrinsic to the human condition; in that sense psychopathology is normal. The task of therapy is not to eliminate suffering but to give a voice to it, to find a form in which it can be expressed. Expression is itself transformation; this is the message that art brings. The therapist then would be an artist of the soul, working with sufferers to enable them to find the proper container for their pain, the form in which it would be embodied. As an artist, the therapist would have to have the power to descend into the Dionysian realm of the unconscious, the chaotic, disordered, obscure (literally, shadowed) part of the mind. Such a perilous journey needs to be supported by a therapeutic community, a group which can "hold" both artist/therapists and sufferers alike.

Often expressive arts therapists work in groups for this very reason; but ultimately, it is the larger community which must support the use of the arts in therapy. Hospitals, clinics, training and academic institutions must become open to the healing function of the arts, and artists themselves must become attuned to the therapeutic implications of their work (as well as its self-healing properties) in order for artist/therapists to have an environment to support them. Perhaps those who employ the arts in psychotherapy will have an effect on others around them as well, opening up their perspectives to new ways of envisioning the world. Perhaps one day there will be a re-unification of the scientific and artistic approaches to mental health, a re-unification in which, as Nietzsche put it, the ideal would be a "Socrates who practices music," healers who can combine rational understanding with artistic sensitivity. For such people to avoid the fate of the historical Socrates, they must have the support of the community in their work. Artists and therapists need to join together to solicit that support. Only then can the therapeutic function of art come into its own.

The Idea of Integration
in the Expressive Arts Therapies

The expresssive arts therapies have, for the most part, developed in a state of relative isolation from each other. In
North America, there are music therapists, dance and movement therapists, art therapists, psychodramatists, drama therapists, play therapists, etc. Each specialty is organized in one
or more associations, with its own standards for certification. There are graduate programs and training institutes
which focus on the different specialities. Each has its own
annual conference, journal, etc. Within this context of
already established specialization, a debate has arisen about
whether expressive arts therapists should be generalists or
specialists, whether they should focus on one particular
discipline or attempt to master several. The debate has
been marked by acrimony and by special-interest pleading.

Because this debate has taken place within a context in
which the specialties dominate the field, the concept of
generalization has been understood to mean the combination of already existing separate entities. A generalist would

be someone who was an art therapist and a music therapist and a drama therapist, etc. He or she would combine different techniques as they were needed. Thus the debate tends to center on the question of whether anyone can really master so many different fields or would only remain on a superficial level in all of them. What has not taken place in this debate is an examination of the central notion of "integration" around which the whole discussion revolves. If integration is understood as putting together what already exists separately, then it can only be understood as a superficial act of generalization which does not alter the essential nature of the parts upon which it operates. We must examine the idea of integration itself in order to see whether it is a dilettante's dream or can really serve as a basis for a transformation of the field.

Integration can be understood philosophically in terms of the age-old debate concerning the relationship of unity and difference. For Plato, each of the Forms or Ideas is already a unification of many particulars; each unifies by being a model for the others to imitate. Ultimately all the forms, by being one or whole, imitate the One, the form of the Good, which is said to be "beyond being" and which enables all the different forms to be. Unity is thus pre-established; what is necessary is to re-call or re-collect this original state of being.

For modern thought, on the other hand, unity lies in the act of unification. It depends upon a prior state of dis-unity or separation. Unity is the integration of a dis-integrated totality, the overcoming of alienation. In Kant and Hegel, in particular, we see this notion of unity as integrative overcoming of difference. For Hegel, identity has already been achieved through the development of speculative reason; for Kant, it is an infinite task which motivates our practical research.

In recent philosophical writing, there has been a reaction against the idealist philosophy of identity. Derrida, in particular, has emphasized the significance of difference as living, creative power in opposition to the dead weight of a reified totality. Adorno's rejection of the philosophy of identity is motivated by a similar repugnance for the false identities of the modern world. The One is understood to be an imperial force crushing the lived reality of particular beings, as the giant modern state crushes the life of its citizens. In psychological thought, James Hillman has spoken of the need for a polytheistic psychology, a psychology in which the forced unity of the ego would give way to a multi-dimensional play of imaginative realities.

This opposition to identity theory has its justification. The homogenization of the world, the disappearance of local cultures and ethnic differences, is mirrored by a homogenization of the self, a flattening of our "infinite variety" into the persona of normality. "One world" usually means that the dominant culture becomes a model for development. Similarly, "identity" most commonly means adjustment to this dominant reality.

I believe, however, that we cannot do without some concept of unity or wholeness. Difference in itself cannot be the basis for a mode of being, political or psychological. The politics of difference founders on the discord and disunity of the many different special-interest groups. It cannot cope with global issues of planetary destruction. Without some vision of the whole, it necessarily degenerates into an assertion of one's own particular well-being, even if that is defined in terms of an excluded group rather than the "compact majority" of Ibsen. And the psychology of difference does not take account of the felt need for unity in the personality, the pain that we feel when we are split or at war with ourselves. Because Hillman rejects the notion of an integral Self, he is ultimately led to give up the idea of therapy altogether: therapy becomes an illusion tied up with the ego's attempt to ground its existence in its own development. For Hillman, there is no self-overcoming, no *Bildung,* only a letting-go into the image that animates our psyche at any particular moment. This would be a Buddhist perspective, if it had a conception of the One that underlies differences. Instead, Hillman rejects the notion of a spiritual psychology and holds fast to his archetypal phenomenology. This method has the danger of becoming a mere description of successive psychic states; instead, it is saved by an implicit faith in the unity of the psyche as creative imagination.

Perhaps this is the point where a return to Kant would be helpful. Kant also sees the imagination as the essence of the soul. The productive imagination, as the art of time, brings the scattered data of the senses together with the formalism of the intellect into a living experience. It is not the image but the act of imagination that unifies and integrates our experience of the world and of the self. This original creative act is to be distinguished from mere fantasy, what Kant calls the "reproductive imagination." Fantasy combines what is already present into novel formations; imagination brings the new into being.

At the same time as each act of imagination is an act of unification or integration, it is also animated by a vision of the whole. For Kant, the soul, the world and God are non-objective totalities which cannot be known in their essence. They remain closed off to us because we literally cannot sense them; there are no sensible data which could make them present, since all sense experience remains partial and limited, whereas these are infinite by definition. This does not, however, mean that they are illusions or that we must retreat into a phenomenalist framework. Rather these infinite totalities become tasks, urging us onwards to greater knowledge of what will always ultimately remain a mystery.

The soul, then, for Kant, is not a psychic entity. It is not a particular experience but the origin or source of experience. It remains forever on the horizon of our experience as that which offers the promise of wholeness. To think that we have understood it scientifically is an illusion based on the reification of a part of its total being. But to think that we do not need a notion of the soul as an idea motivating our research is absurd. Without it, the drive towards self-knowledge would be inexplicable.

Heidegger takes up Kant's idea of a non-objective ground in his notion of "Being." The ontological difference between Being and beings, of which Heidegger speaks, means that we can never have an objective knowledge of our essence. Indeed, our essence is to be that which utters the word of Being. We dwell poetically on the earth insofar as we surrender to the ground of our being by bringing forth what is in speech. Here Heidegger echoes Kant's emphasis on the creative imagination: *poiesis* or *Dichtung* (poetry) is the timely word that lets Being be. *Dasein* (human being) unifies the fourfold, bringing together heaven and earth, gods and mortals, through the primal leap *(Ursprung)* that binds our history with our power-to-be in the coming-to-presence of what is.

Heidegger's notion of Being is clearly distinguished from the idea of a One that would deny or obliterate differences. In fact, Heidegger identifies this latter notion with the God of the metaphysical tradition. His deconstruction of that tradition liberates the poetic imagination as the source of human experience. This implies that human being is creative in its essence. We do not first satisfy our basic needs and then in our spare time, if we have any, entertain ourselves with artistic pursuits. Or rather, we may in fact do that, but in so doing, we forget who we are: the poetic being par excellence.

What relationship do these philosophical issues bear to the problem of integration in expressive arts therapy? Even if we grant that integration is central to human existence, we still must justify its role within the therapeutic enterprise and within arts therapy in particular. I believe, in fact, that we can use this notion to comprehend the process of expressive arts therapy.

Integration implies a previous state of dis-integration. Often, what brings a person into therapy is the experience of falling apart, of splitting into discordant fragments, of losing a central self around which the personality coheres. This break-down is a necessary stage in the development of the self: it represents the breaking down of the false unity of narcissistic self-identification. A crisis has occurred which cannot be met by the old persona. The person is plunged into disarray; he or she loses the certainty of their former stable identity. There is an experience of the void, of a loss of meaning and purpose. Yeats describes it well: "Things fall apart; the center cannot hold; Mere anarchy is loosed upon the world". Dabrowski calls this "positive dis-integration"; it is the necessary prelude to growth.

At this point, typically, what the person wants most is to go back to the old ways, to find the comfort and security of a former manner of being. He or she clings desperately to the image of a former self and will deny, if possible, any need to give it up. Here the therapist's intervention is crucial. If he or she has not gone through a similar process, it will be tempting to collaborate with the person in going back to the former identity. We could call this a "regressive restoration of the persona". But if therapists are aware of their own process, they will be willing to suffer the discomfort of letting clients go through the experience of disintegration. Their caring for clients will be demonstrated by a willingness to be there for them and to let the process happen without interference. Heidegger calls this "authentic care", as opposed to the inauthentic kind which is not willing to let others be but must leap in and correct their being. It is the therapists' own fear of breaking down that prevents them from letting clients go through the experience of disintegration.

The therapeutic act consists of "being-with" clients as they go through their suffering. "Empathy" and "unconditional positive regard" are other terms we use to describe this kind of care. It seems we need the help of others in order to be ourselves.

A good description of the entire process is found in Tolstoy's *The Death of Ivan Ilych*. Ivan Ilych is a bureaucrat who identifies with the image of himself that he presents to others. When he discovers that he has an incurable disease and will soon die, he finds that this image is powerless to give his life meaning. His world disintegrates and he experiences himself face-to-face with nothingness. What gives him the power to accept his fate is the care of a young peasant boy, who lets him rest his feet on his shoulders to relieve the pain. This beautiful story presents the process of healing in all its phases: narcissistic self-identification, crisis and break-down, recovery and the restoration of the self.

It is essential to realize that the restored self is different from the initial identity. The person is now identified not with the ego or the persona but with the ground of his or her being. Whether this ground be called the "unconscious" or "God", it is clear that what has taken place is an integration of the personality on a deeper foundation. It is a movement towards wholeness and unity.

Given this description of the therapeutic process, what role can expressive arts therapists play? In the first place, it is important to see that the stages of the therapeutic and creative processes are essentially the same. Artists must go through a similar experience of breaking down the stabilized form which they face. Creation depends upon destruction, a willingness to give up a previous pattern and to experiment with a new form. Letting-go, the experience of emptiness and the emergence of the new characterize the creative as well as the therapeutic processes. Similarly one could speak of therapy as a creative act; the suffering individual creates a new self out of the ashes of the old. The therapist facilitates this creative process. In this sense, all therapy is creative in its essence.

But in addition arts therapists use the disciplines of art to help a person go through his or her process. Art gives a voice to suffering. It expresses the pain and confusion of the disintegration of the self, and, in so doing, enables clients to face themselves without reservation. To dance suffering, to paint it or put it into poetic form is to confront it directly and to give oneself up to it. In this expressive moment, one lets go of attachment to the former security and is willing to face the void. At such times, images of wholeness may arise, symbols which express the possible resolution of the crisis. By enabling the person to express his or her suffering, the arts therapist gives them the possibility of transcending it. Art then can be both a cry of despair in the night as well as a triumphant hosanna of joy.

The arts are pathways or methods that take us deeper into ourselves and our experience. As we enter unreservedly into the depth of ourselves, we encounter healing energies and experience the hope of integration. Though this ultimate wholeness is never given to us, it remains a vision that animates our work on ourselves. It is an infinite task in Kant's sense of the term.

The expressive arts therapies are integrative by nature. What, then, are we to make of the disintegrated state of the field? One might be tempted to view it in analogy to the therapeutic process itself. Each discipline clings narcissistically to its own idealized image, refusing to acknowledge the pain of separation and disunity that exists in the field as a whole. When attempts are made to bring the separate parts together, each wants to hold on to its own identity so as not to lose the comfort and security that it has achieved. As a result, these attempts at integration remain superficial. They take place from the top down rather than from the bottom up and never reach the foundations. There is an awareness of crisis; but it is dealt with by holding on to the old identity and seeing change as threatening. This process is manifested in the desire to become more professional, to raise standards of certification and to gain legitimacy in the eyes of others.

In the end, the arts run the risk of becoming techniques, to be utilized according to standard operating procedures. Client diagnoses, treatment methods and outcome studies all conform to this reified conception of therapeutic practice. Arts therapists become "mental health professionals" and seek to have the status and income that they feel they deserve. Ironically, their role as specialized technicians keeps them in an adjunctive position, to be used in special or difficult cases under the supervision of the "real" professionals, the psychiatrists. Their very attempt at legitimacy makes them illegitimate as therapists, poor relations to be treated condescendingly and without respect.

The solution is not to call for another conference where the separate arts therapists will speak to each other of their isolation. Rather it is necessary for every one of us to re-think the foundations of our work. What does it mean to be human? What causes suffering? What is therapy? What role can the arts play in the therapeutic process? These are the questions that will help us understand the nature of expressive arts therapy and the extent to which the current organization of the field expresses or distorts this nature.

As we touch upon the roots of our own work, we will also find the common foundation that will enable us to communicate authentically with each other. Integration in the field of expressive arts therapy depends upon each individual therapist experiencing the process of break-down and healing through creative action. What we have in common is our humanity: the poetic imagination that enables us to express and thereby surmount our suffering. Poiesis brings us together; as long as we remain within this common dimension, we can share a vision of integration. The community of expressive arts therapists depends upon the sharing of this vision.

The Play of Imagination

On the Possibility of Expressive Therapy

What makes expressive arts therapy possible? Expressive therapy presupposes that the arts can be therapeutic. How is it that artistic expression can have a healing function within a therapeutic context? To frame the question in this way is to undertake a critique, in the Kantian sense.

Kant's *Critique of Pure Reason* begins with the assumption that Newtonian physics is a valid way of obtaining objective truth about the natural world. Kant assumes the validity of natural science and asks, how is this knowledge possible, i.e., what is it in the constitution of the human mind that enables us to have such knowledge? In a similar fashion, I am assuming the validity of expressive therapy. I assume that it "works", that in fact there is a healing process that uses artistic expression as its medium. I am not then attempting to demonstrate its efficacy but rather to understand the conditions of its possibility.

This effort requires that I pose some fundamental questions regarding the constitution of human existence. What is the nature of the psyche? What is psychological suffering? What does it mean to heal this suffering? How can the arts be a means of such healing? Under what conditions does artistic expression become therapeutic?

These are "big" questions which leave me aware of the limitations of my knowledge. Nevertheless, they are questions which must receive some answer, else the entire enterprise of expressive therapy would be carried out without any basic understanding. If nothing else, each practitioner must find his or her own answer to make sense of their work.

I would like to sketch out some directions for answering these questions by looking at a parallel development in psychological and philosophical thinking. I believe there has been a convergence in these two disciplines which points the way toward a deeper understanding of our work. Using Winnicott and Heidegger as key figures, I will try to show the new understanding of human existence that may help to serve as a basis for therapeutic practice.

To begin with Winnicott means to go back to Freud and Winnicott's place in the psychoanalytic tradition. As I have indicated earlier in this book, Freud's own thinking demonstrates a profound ambivalence about the meaning of artistic expression in psychological life. Freud was a cultivated man, widely read in classical literature. He kept up an interest in the cultural life of his time and was familiar with many artists and writers. His works are laden with literary references. The central metaphor of his thinking, the Oedipus complex, owes its origin, of course, to a literary source. Freud wrote many articles on the artistic process and devoted a great deal of effort to understanding it. He often praised artists, along with scientists, as the only ones capable of sublimating instinctual drives without losing psychic energy. One tendency of Freud's thinking, then, is to see art as a means to psychological health and the artist as a higher type of human being.

At the same time, however, Freud exhibited a profound suspicion of and distrust toward artists and art-works. Artists are depicted as day-dreamers, incapable of taking action in the real world. They are somehow too weak constitutionally for the trials of reality; in compensation, they take refuge in a fantasy life in which they imagine the instinctual satisfaction that is missing in actual experience. If they are lucky, the rewards of their work may include the pleasures that they were only able to dream about. But whether successful or not, artists create without real awareness of what they are doing. The deeper meaning of their work is only available to a scientific observer. The work must be interpreted for its unconscious meaning, and that can only be done by one who is familiar with the laws of psychological experience, the psychoanalyst.

This ambivalence in Freud has been noted before. Paul Ricoeur, in particular, has pointed out the tension in Freud's work between "archaeological" and "teleological" explanations, between reductive and expansive approaches to the psyche, between what Ricoeur calls a hermeneutic of suspicion and a hermeneutic of generosity. The source of this ambivalence, on a theoretical level, stems from the peculiar nature of Freud's discoveries.

On the one hand, Freud, as a medical doctor and natural scientist, identified himself as a child of the Enlightenment. He wanted to find a rational explanation for mental life. His task was to order the chaos of experience and discover the basic principles which render it comprehensible. Such knowledge can lead to practical efficacy. Only if we find a science of the psyche can we have an effective means of treating its dysfunctions.

On the other hand, the subject matter of Freud's work resists rational explanation. In particular, the unconscious, as the basis of mental life, is irrational; it rejects the law of contradiction and mixes together fragments of experience with fantasy, memory and desire. This means that the soul is fundamentally inimical to rational comprehension. Freud's greatness is that he never ceased to seek for scientific understanding while at the same time he constantly held on to the irrational nature of the psyche. He was thus able to keep the tension between Enlightenment and Romantic tendencies of knowing. This is in part why disparate interpretations of Freud are possible and why psychoanalysis itself has been able to split into contrary directions.

One such direction is the object-relations school of British psychoanalysis, based on the work of Melanie Klein. There are many ways to characterize this school; like every other intellectual movement, it has a certain style which is readily identifiable. For our purposes, what is most important in object-relations is the emphasis on the early fantasy life of the child.

The term "object-relations" itself is profoundly misleading. No matter how much we remind ourselves of the strict definition of "object" as that to which a drive (sexual or aggressive) is attached, we are constantly tempted to think of a real object (or person) and a real relation. Object-relations then turns into an interpersonal theory.

What is missing in this interpretation of object-relations theory is the role of fantasy. The "object" is not the other; it is an internal representation of the other to which my psychic energy is attached or "cathected"; that is to say, the object is an image of what I am attached to. In a strict Kleinian formulation, I never have a relationship to the real other (primarily the mother); rather I dwell in an internal fantasy world of mental representations. The other is there for me only as represented within this internal sphere.

Klein is following one tendency of Freud's thinking here. Within the modern conception of the mind to which Freud adhered, there is a gap between subject and object which can only be bridged by mental representations. The instincts for Freud always express themselves in derivative forms as representations; they are never experienced directly. Thus the mind-body split of modern thinking makes psychoanalysis into a science of mental life purely, a study of the internal world of the subject. This produces a gap between internal and external reality which tends to keep analysis within the consulting-room and renders behavioural change problematical.

What is interesting is that for Freud, in contrast to Descartes, the founder of modern thought, the internal world is not a world of thoughts but of images. Mental life is imaginal not rational. Klein was able to take this insight and use it in her development of play therapy with children. Childrens' play is seen as an expression of their internal mental states. The child analyst must interpret the play to find the child's "object-relations", i.e., the internal fantasy world shaped by his or her drives.

Although Winnicott situates himself in this tradition and uses much of its terminology, he is the first analyst to begin to break out of the presuppositions which shape the discoveries of psychoanalysis into a pre-determined form. He follows Klein in acknowledging the importance of childrens' play and fantasy life; but he situates this discovery in a radically new framework through his notion of transitional space.

Winnicott's discussion of the transitional object, that blanket or other thing which is in between the self and the world is well-known. The transitional object is both me and not-me; it is neither internal not external but serves as a bridge or connector between both realms. Developmentally, it is found when the child is able to begin to move out of merger with the mother and before he or she has attained a sense of individual selfhood. Winnicott's concept is familiar to us; but I do not know how aware we are of the radical implications which it contains.

For Winnicott, the transitional object and the transitional space in which it appears are at the center of psychological life. Transitional phenomena are not just interesting occurrences in a sequence of developmental steps. Rather they express the central characteristic of mental life: the psyche is not inside nor is it outside; it is in-between. Psychological life is transitional. That is to say, healthy psychological experience takes place in transitional space; it is only in illness that we wall ourselves up in an interior world. And, similarly, it is only in the flight from illness that we deny the very existence of interiority and take refuge in a "real" world outside us.

Winnicott discovered transitional space through the *experience* of play. I emphasize the word "experience" to distinguish Winnicott's relationship to play from Klein's. For Klein, ultimately, the analyst's role is to stand outside and watch the child at play; this gives the analyst the objectivity necessary to understand the child's internal experience. Interpretation then is the key to penetrating into this inner subjective realm. The subject-object split on which Klein's theory relies makes it impossible for her to recognize the transitional nature of play.

Winnicott, on the other hand, is always playing *with* the child, even when he is merely present. That is, he never becomes a disinterested observer, outside of the field of play. Rather, the therapeutic space is understood as playground, a place where both patient and analyst are involved. In this space, interpretation cannot come from "outside", if there is to be interpretation at all. Instead, it must come from within the transitional world in which both analyst and patient play.

The nature of this kind of interpretation would itself be an interesting and important thing to study. In some ways it would seem to be closer to literary interpretation than the explanations of natural science. Just as literary interpretation is itself a part of literature, so interpretation within transitional space would have to partake of the playful, involved character of that space. The boundary between interpretation and play would itself be permeable and shifting.

Winnicott's conception of transitional space challenges our understanding of the role of the imagination in psychotherapy. What happens to fantasy when it is no longer "inside"; i.e., when there is no longer a presumption that the world is accessible only through mental representations? Winnicott makes a clear distinction between "fantasy" and "imagination". Fantasy is imagination *manqué;* it refers to the kind of day-dreaming that walls the person up in his or her internal world and leads to no form of doing, of efficacity. Imagination, on the other hand, is the means by which we reach out and connect with otherness. Play, then, is the operation of imagination not of fantasy. In a certain sense, we could say that the goal of therapy is to replace fantasy with imagination, to transform psychological space from an isolated, lifeless world of private obsessions into a connected, vital field of play. Therapy then can be understood to be a re-vitalization of the imagination, a turning-back to an original connection between self and world.

Again, it is essential to understand the mediating role of imagination here. We are not contrasting an "inner" realm of fantasy with an "outer" world of reality; this is precisely the dichotomy that gives rise to the split between Enlightenment and Romantic models of psychotherapy. What Winnicott is saying, implicitly, is that psychic life is imaginal; we live in the imaginative and playful space of experience.

There is a convergence here with Jung, especially in the interpretation of Jung which James Hillman provides. Hillman reminds us that Jung once said that "psyche is image", that the basic form of psychological process is an imaginative one. Hillman's recent turn from clinical work to a wider political perspective, searching for the *anima mundi,* the soul in and of the world, is another attempt to bridge the gap which modern thought has left us. If the psyche is imaginal, then it is in the world, not outside of it in a private space. When psychological experience is cut off from connnection to a world of others, we suffer from this loss. Psychopathology results from an injury to our imaginative capacity.

Winnicott's notion of the in-between character of mental life is especially interesting for the light which it sheds upon psychopathology. For Winnicott, the suffering of the soul comes from the split between self and world. The child's primary creativity, if inadequately mirrored by those who care for him or her, is driven inward. The child then protects his or her sense of aliveness, of being, by turning away from those who would deny it into an internal, protected realm. A false, compliant self is presented to others; the "true" self is protected inside. The alternatives become either a lifeless routinized existence in the false self or an impotent, withdrawn life in fantasy.

The implication of Winnicott's view is that the subject-object split which underlies traditional psychoanalytic thinking is itself pathological. This split arises out of illness; a theory which reproduces it cannot adequately account for the overcoming of illness in therapeutic work. Thus we need a new formulation of human existence which can help us understand how the psyche can become whole, healthy, and alive, how it can find its vitality through participation in the world.

Here is where a turn to Heidegger may be helpful. Heidegger's thinking is based on a critique of the subject-object split and an attempt to understand the person as a being-in-the-world. Of course, Heidegger and Winnicott inhabit different universes of discourse; there is no question of a simple equation of the one with the other. On the other hand, as Heidegger's follower Gadamer has shown, different language games are always capable of some form of mediation and translation. We are thus looking for that space "in-between" Winnicott and Heidegger which can form a vital connection between them. Gadamer calls this the "fusion of horizons" and suggests that it is the basis of all true understanding.

To begin with, then, the central notion in Heidegger's book, *Being and Time,* is that human existence, what Heidegger calls *Dasein,* or being-there, cannot be understood within the Cartesian framework of subject and object. For human being to have the character of existence, to be capable of being-there, means that human being is always in-the-world. *Dasein* does not first exist and then come to be in a world. Rather, it is essential to *Dasein* that it be worldly.

Heidegger illustrates this notion by a phenomenological analysis of ordinary, everyday being-in-the-world, in which we go about our concerns and try to achieve our goals. We find ourselves first and foremost occupied with the world. Worldly existence is primary; the split into becoming detached observers of an "objective" world that stands over against us occurs only when our purposes are frustrated, when something doesn't "work". Then we step back and try to understand the thing in question; at that point it ceases to be something to use and becomes an object of our understanding. Everyday existence is thus mundane existence, being-in-a-world.

However, the primacy of ordinary, everyday being-in-the-world does not mean that we are always being ourselves in the world. On the contrary, in Heidegger's view, we are primarily in the world in an inauthentic way, caught up in the daily round, subject to the sway of what he terms *"Das Man"*, the anonymous social sphere of what "one" does, says or thinks. It is only when we suffer from the anxiety that comes with an awareness of our own finitude, the fact that we will die, that we realize that we essentially do not belong to the "one".

Death individualizes; confronted with my own mortality, I can no longer rely on what "one" does, for no one else can take on my own death. In grasping myself as a being-toward-death, I assume the responsibility of living my own life as well. This means accepting who I am and choosing to live out the possibilities that are authentically my own, not those pre-arranged for me by others. Authentic existence comes when *Dasein* experiences the dread that comes with an awareness of his or her finitude and resolves to be who they are by casting forward into the future those authentic possibilities which arise from what they have been.

Casting a glance back at Winnicott, we can see an essential affinity with this aspect of Heidegger's thought. The worldly character of *Dasein* is akin to the transitional space of which Winnicott speaks. Just as authentic *Dasein* is in the world, so psychological life for Winnicott is carried out in the transitional space between self and other.

Furthermore, Winnicott's distinction between the true and false self-systems is similar to Heidegger's distinction between authentic and inauthentic existence. Inauthentic existence is that in which I am hidden from myself. It is only in the experience of break-down, when the comfort of normality no longer suffices, that I can find my own truth. To live according to *Das Man* is to be compliant with what I believe to be the expectations of others. At the same time, it is to choose not to be, to live a half-life in which I do not confront the terror or experience the joy of existence.

Heidegger, like Winnicott, is not saying that the true or authentic self is to be found in an interior space. This is the Romantic view which gives rise to a literature of inwardness. This turning inward, moreover, is also a movement toward pathology. Nor is Heidegger saying that authenticity is to be found "outside", as is asserted in Enlightenment conceptions of external reality and in everyday notions of normal, healthy living. Rather, the authentic self is in the world; i.e., it grasps those possibilities which are to be found in what is actual and it casts them forward as its own.

This act of "projection" of my ownmost possibilities (and here Heidegger is clearly using "projection" in a different sense than the psychoanalytic one) is essentially an act of vision or insight. Projection is the imaginative capacity for seeing the possible in the actual. This connection of authenticity with imagination, implicit in *Being and Time,* becomes a central feature of Heidegger's thinking in his later writings. When we ask what kind of existence is authentic existence, Heidegger's ultimate answer is that it is "poetic" existence. He is referring here not primarily to poetry in the sense of written verse but to poetry as the imaginative capacity for envisioning and speaking one's own authentic truth.

"Poetically man dwells on the earth"; Heidegger takes this statement of Hölderlin's and interprets it to mean that we find our home in the world only when we can imagine it to be our own, only when we have transformed it into an authentic dwelling-place. Heidegger calls this transformative activity "poiesis" or *"Dichtung"*, "poetry" in the sense in which Shelley called the poets the unacknowledged legislators of mankind: those who bring-forth into the world that which truly is. Because human being is essentially poetic, the arts are seen by Heidegger as ways in which truth happens or comes to be.

For the later Heidegger, poiesis is an essential way of the happening of truth, a place in which truth comes to take a stand. Poiesis is that act by which truth is placed in a work; it is the casting forward of new possibilities of being-in-the-world which are then held or contained in an art-work. Authentic existence for Heidegger is poetic existence. Rilke once said that *"Gesang ist Dasein"*, song is existence; we could interpret Heidegger as transposing that statement to read, *"Dasein ist Gesang"*, existence is essentially poetic.

The convergence here with Winnicott's thinking should be obvious. For Winnicott, to be alive is to be capable of being creative; the essential self-assertion of children is to affirm their own existence in the world through creative living. Play is the means of expression of our creativity. When we lose the capacity for imaginative life, for play, then we "die" to ourselves, we experience a living death which is often masked by a compliant outer shell. For Heidegger, authentic existence is poetic existence; it is the affirmation of my ownmost possibilities in the world. When I forget my capacity to dwell poetically, I lose myself as well. I become caught up in the social whirl, in flight from the anxiety of being alive, of being mortal.

Both Winnicott and Heidegger see the necessity for what I would call "healing" in a process of re-covery of the true or authentic self. I must somehow turn back to myself and find again what I have never truly lost: the creative ground of my being. What distinguishes Winnicott from Heidegger is in the conception of what makes such a turn possible. In

Being and Time, Heidegger seems to be saying that authenticity requires a process of individualization. Not only is it the case that I must become myself, but it is also true that I must do so by myself.

Heidegger's image of the authentic self in his early writings has a heroic cast; it is the image of a solitary individual who by his or her own resolve faces the ultimate terror of death and accepts their fate. Although Heidegger names being-with-others as an essential characteristic of *Dasein,* others are depicted primarily as members of the anonymous mass. I must separate myself from them in order to become authentic. Only after I have done so can I undertake an authentic being-with-others; only then can we form a genuine community.

The only place where this general tendency in Heidegger seems to be overcome is when he talks about authentic care or "solitude", a caring which frees the other for his or her own possibilities as opposed to stepping in and taking over for them. However it is not at all clear how this authentic care can serve in the quest for authenticity. Rather authenticity seems to be the precondition for solitude. Only if I can be true to myself can I authentically care for others; but does my caring for them then help them in their own search for authenticity? It is difficult to see how this is possible on Heidegger's premises. The possibility of therapeutic action remains obscure.

In Heidegger's later work, belongingness to a tradition becomes more central than the process of individualization. The possibilities that are my own are those which have been given me by others. To take them up is to continue the tradition in which I stand. For Heidegger it is the "creators", those who have dwelt poetically in the world and brought truth into a work, who leave genuine possibilities for the ones who come after. We can, even in an inauthentic world, at least learn to be "preservers" of the truth that remains. Thus I can only stand in the truth that others have given to me. Finding my own truth means finding my connection to the living tradition to which I belong. Nevertheless, it is still unclear how others can help us find this connection.

For Winnicott, on the other hand, the role of the other in the development of the self is central. Only after the experience of unity with the mother is the child capable of emerging into the transitional space of creativity. If children have not been able to bond or merge with the mother, they will be unable to begin to separate. They will tend to stay in symbiosis or flee into independence as a defense against fears of engulfment. In either case, their capacity for creative living in the world will be damaged.

Similarly, the therapeutic process is only possible in Winnicott's view if the therapist can foster the patient's creative life. The therapist needs to be able to find a way to help the patient dwell in the transitional space that they share. That is, he or she needs to be able to help the patient to play. In Winnicott's thinking, the presence of the other is essential for the development of my own creativity. Winnicott's formulations acknowledge the essential dependence of human beings upon one another. I can only become myself in relationship.

And yet even in Winnicott there is an acknowledgement of the limits of being with others. He talks of an unapproachable core of selfhood in each person, a part of the self that can never be fully shared. The therapist must accept this unapproachable core of the person and not try to penetrate into it. Even in the transitional space of psychotherapy as creative play, there is an essential aloneness which can never be fully shared. We can only sense its presence and show our respect by letting it be.

Winnicott and Heidegger share an important insight into the limits of understanding. I can never completely grasp the essence of the other. For this reason, my interpretations can never be authoritative. I am not "outside" the other looking "in"; I am not the detached observer of another's psychological process. Rather we share the same space; we are involved with one another. Paradoxically, this very proximity keeps us apart. Sharing does not mean merging. Nor can I expect to find a truth from my perspective that can be taken over by another; rather we must engage in a mutual quest for truth, a truth "in between". This truth is neither subjective nor objective; it is the living expression of our being together in the world. For this reason, we must constantly create it anew.

What can this comparison of Winnicott and Heidegger tell us regarding the possibility of expressive therapy? In the first place, by freeing us from the subject-object split of modern thought, it enables us to understand the central role of the imagination in psychological life. If we are isolated subjects detached from objects, then the image is only an internal representation of an external world. Only a reflective consciousness could then tell if the image gives us a true picture of reality or a false one. This would mean that the truth is restricted to analytical knowledge. Imagination would give us at best likenesses, imitations of the real.

Within this framework, imagination is necessary only because of our accidental status as embodied beings. Embodiment is seen as implying a confusion of mental and extended substances, mind and matter. Analytical intelligence must act as if it were "nowhere", as if it were able to assume a perspective outside of any particular embodied being. From this perspective it can see into the "true" nature of the object without the distortion of the senses.

Imagination, on the other hand, is always embodied thinking. It carries a thought within an image, a thought which cannot be detached from the image without losing its vitality. Within the framework of subject-object thinking, the imagination is an enemy to truth. It distorts the clarity and distinctness of the concept by presenting it in sensible form.

If we, however, following Heidegger and Winnicott, are able to transcend the framework of subject-object thinking and conceive of human being as being-in-the-world, then the imagination becomes central to our understanding of experience. Imagination is the medium of mental or psychological life. To be alive means to be in the world as embodied beings, capable of imagining ourselves more deeply, i.e., seeing our authentic possibilities in the course of our lives. This distinguishes imagination from fantasy, which ignores actuality in constructing images of pleasure or pain. Imagination can be said to be the "bridge" between self and world; but we must remember that we are always "on" this bridge. When we try to pass to one side or the other, we "fall" into the chasm of fantasy.

This preeminence of the imagination means that living and living creatively are the same. We are in the world in a vital way only through creative affirmation, the imaginative projection of our own possibilities. Sickness and suffering, then, come from a wound to our imaginative capacity. We fantasize because we cannot imagine. Through fear of rejection and abandonment, we detach ourselves from our bodies, from others, from the world as a whole.

Though patients seem to be living in a world of imagination, it is in fact their imagination which has been injured. They have lost the capacity to be in the world in a creative way. Healing does not mean bringing them back to "reality"; this would be to flip to the other side of their split experience of life. There is no reality that is actual, i.e., alive, without embodied imagination, the capacity to see otherwise.

Instead, healing has to be understood as the restoration of a person's imaginative capacity. Only the restoration of the imagination will heal our souls. This restoration takes place through the creation of an imaginal space between therapist and patient. The therapist must find a way to invite the patient into this shared imaginal space. In this space, in which both patient and therapist are involved, therapeutic play can take place. This also, and even sometimes, primarily, means experiencing the barriers to play. The therapist must affirm resistance as a strategy for survival of the self, while, at the same time, inviting the patient to enter the transitional space between them.

The play of imagination always requires a medium, some form which can serve as a bridge between self and other. Here is where the particular virtue of expressive arts therapy becomes evident. The arts, as media of the imagination, are disciplines which give form and substance to our capacity to be who we are. Each artistic medium embodies the imagination in a concrete and specific way. Through the use of sound, movement, visual image and dramatic enactment, I imaginatively express my being-in-the-world.

Expressive therapy is possible, then, because life is imaginal. The wound to the imagination can only be healed by the aid of the imagination. The therapist's affirmation of the patient's creative life restores the connection to what has been lost. Thus only a theory of human existence which acknowledges the essential role of the imagination can provide an adequate basis for understanding the possibility of expressive therapy.

Poiesis makes healing possible. Psychotherapy must hold fast to this insight if it wishes to be authentic. We do not aim at helping someone adapt to reality; rather we seek to help him or her live more creatively. Only the restoration of the imagination can achieve this goal. The possibility of expressive therapy lies in the play of imagination. This is a truth which can only be thought by being lived.

Bearing Gifts to the Feast

The Presentation as a Rite of Passage in the Education of Expressive Therapists

How does someone become an expressive arts therapist? That is, how does a person who is interested in psychotherapy and the arts undergo a transformation into becoming a healing artist, capable of placing artistic media in the service of the soul? In this paper, I would like to talk about one way of effecting this transformation, a way that I use in training students at York University in Toronto. I call this method the "presentation." It is a modification of a process that I first learned when studying with Paolo Knill at Lesley College in Cambridge, Ma.

In discussing the presentation, I will try to think about its general significance for the education of expressive therapists. I believe that the principles involved in the presentation are manifest in some form wherever this kind of education occurs. To understand these principles, I will draw on the anthropological literature concerning rites of passage and gift exchange. My essential point is that the presentation is a rite of passage in becoming gifted as an expressive arts therapist.

First, I would like to describe this process. In my classes at York, each student is required to make a presentation to the rest of the group. The requirement for the presentation is simply that the student must present some issue or conflict in his or her life and that the issue must be presented through one or more artistic media. I meet with students beforehand to help them formulate the structure of the presentation. At the end of each presentation, the group gives feedback to the presenter. Initial feedback can take the form of verbal responses, beginning with the words, "I feel...", "I imagine..." or I remember...". Subsequent feedback however, must itself be in an expressive mode, i.e., it must use an artistic or expressive medium. Each presenter, in particular, is responsible for giving expressive feedback to the student who presents next. After the presentation is complete, including feedback, the student must write a process report, in which he or she reflects on the process involved in doing the presentation and receiving feedback. The process report includes description, interpretation and evaluation of the process of presenting. The presentation is complete when I return the process with my own written response.

I call this process a "presentation" for several reasons. First of all, students are presenting something; they are making something manifest to the group. In fact, what they are presenting is themselves; they are showing the pain and suffering in their lives. In presenting in this way, secondly, the student must become present. The suffering that he or she is presenting must be made actual in the here and now; it must be re-enacted and re-lived. Moreover, the student is there with others who themselves must be present to meet with him or her. They must be acutely attuned to their own felt responses in order to join with the presenter in the way that he or she needs. Thirdly, the presence of the student is itself a present, that is, a gift; it is a gift offered to the group to which the group responds by offering feedback, gifts in exchange.

When the presentation works, and it does not always work, both the presenter and the group become authentically present to each other and to themselves. The normal masks and defenses that we use to hide behind and protect ourselves are dropped. We face each other as suffering souls. This communion gives us the sense of a community; what we have in common is our vulnerability and our willingness to confront it openly.

Two things are necessary for the presentation to work. First, the presenter must be willing to present his or her pain to the group. What they need to show is their "psychopathology", in the original root meaning of the word, i.e., a logos of the pathos of the psyche, a telling of the suffering of the soul. If the presenter does not tell this story, if he or she presents something superficial or peripheral instead of deep and central, then they will not be authentically present, and nothing will happen in the class.

But secondly, the story must be told through the arts in order for the presentation to be effective. The reason for this is that the arts "make-present"; they re-create in the living moment a suffering that has been. If the presenter "talks about" his or her suffering instead of putting it into artistic form, it remains distant from us; it is not actualized in the here and now. On the other hand, when the moment of pain is re-created in an artistic form, then it becomes real; we feel as if it were occurring for the first time. We cannot help but be affected or moved by it.

Over the course of the last several years, I have seen presentations of the most diverse sorts. Students have presented all sorts of wounds, from abuse and rejection by parents or other care-takers to abandonment by God. Similarly, the most diverse media have been utilized: visual art, dance/movement, music and vocalization, psychodrama and other dramatic forms, performance art, mask, puppetry, etc. Simple materials, like the elements of earth, water and fire are sometimes brought in. Often, members of the group are asked to assist in the presentation. Sometimes I intervene at the student's request, when he or she feels "stuck".

To give an example, a recurring theme in the presentations has been the "wall": a student feels barriers between him or herself and others, they are unable to achieve intimacy due to fears of rejection or absorption. In several presentations in different classes, students have spontaneously chosen this theme and constructed various types of barriers or blockades between themselves and members of the group. The "wall" then becomes present in the here and now as group members are asked to choose whether to approach it and themselves risk rejection or to stay outside and face their own isolation.

Sometimes presentations are extremely dramatic; they involve strong physical expressions of feeling and invoke dramatic responses in return. At other times, presentations are quiet and subtle, yet their effect is equally powerful. What is most interesting is the variety and uniqueness of the presentations; each, when authentic, seems to be a unique expression of the soul of the presenter. Each brings a new energy and a new form into the group. There is a hidden beauty in every presenter which springs forth during the presentation. The manifestation of this beauty brings joy and grace to the group as a whole.

In these classes, students are required to do other work besides presentations. Each student must conduct a self-exploration through artistic media, involving at least six one-hour sessions. Subsequently, students must form pairs and take turns guiding each other's process of self-exploration, again for a minimum of six hour-long sessions. These explorations result in process reports which reflect upon and integrate the experiences involved. Often this work becomes the basis for the presentation, or else the presentation is used as a starting-point for further exploration in the sessions. In addition, there are group exercises designed to introduce expressive therapy techniques and to build trust in the group so that students will feel free to present at their deepest and most vulnerable level. Students also keep journals in which to reflect upon, both expressively and discursively, the relation of the class to their own process. But the focus of the class is on the presentation. It is as if the presentation were the key to becoming an expressive therapist. Of course, most of these students will not make the choice of expressive therapy as a career; but for some of them this is the point at which their vocation becomes evident. I would now like to situate the presentation within the context of the theory of rites of passage in order to try to understand how it can be so effective.

Arnold van Gennep published his classic text, *Les rites de passage,* in 1908. Van Gennep was one of a number of brilliant French sociologists, including Emile Durkheim and Marcel Mauss, who rejected the prevailing British approach to social phenomena which sought to comprehend their evolutionary or developmental significance. Instead the French school tried to give an analysis of the morphological structure of a social fact, its form, in order to provide a dynamic schema which could account for its diverse manifestation.

In the case of van Gennep, the social facts to be explained are the rituals or ceremonies which mark the transition from one group to another. In any society, individuals pass from group to group in the course of their lives: from unborn to born, from child to adult, from unmarried to married, from the living to the dead. A person undergoing a change in social status is considered to be sacred or set apart; he or she has to be re-incorporated in the group with the new status. Rituals or ceremonies which connect the sacred with the profane effect the passage from one group to another. These rituals of passage, then, are what van Gennep seeks to understand.

In accordance with the method of the French school of sociology at that time, van Gennep does not attempt to trace the historical development of these rituals. Nor does he inquire into their religious or psychological significance. Instead he seeks to find what he calls the underlying "schéma", the categorical form which can generate all the diverse types of rite. He finds this form through an analysis of what he cails the "territorial passage", the journey from one country or region to another. In every such passage, an individual must leave his own territory, pass through a neutral zone and finally enter another territory. The passage between the two regions, van Gennep calls a "transition" *(marge)*. It is this element of transition which characterizes all the rituals of passage which he wishes to explain.

The underlying *schéma* for these rituals has three elements: *séparation, marge, agrégation,* that is separation, transition and incorporation. Every rite of passage is characterized by these three phases. In addition, there are particular rituals for each phase. Since passage involves crossing an entranceway or threshold (Latin, *limin*) into a new world, van Gennep distinguishes between "pre-liminal", "liminal" and "post-liminal" rites. Different passages will stress different types of ritual; for example, "rites of separation are prominent in funeral ceremonies, rites of incorporation at marriages. Transition rites may play an important part...in...initiation."[1]

The state of transition is in fact central for van Gennep. As in the territorial passage in which the traveller must journey through the no-man's land between countries, every social passage involves a journey into a symbolic region where one is no longer a member of the old group and not yet a member of the new. In this state, the individual loses his or her previous status; they are, in a sense, "dead", having lost their earlier social life and not yet acquired a new one. In order to enter their new condition, they must be "re-born". For van Gennep, every rite of passage involves a symbolic death and re-birth. This is particularly evident in initiation rites, in which the "novices are considered dead during the trial period...The initiates act as if they were newly born."[2]

In focusing on the idea of symbolic death and re-birth, van Gennep transcends his categorical framework. Here he is not only generating a *schéma* to explain a variety of social facts; he is also interpreting the significance of these facts. Rites of passage accomplish personal and social regeneration through symbolic death and re-birth. In van Gennep's own words, "life itself means to separate and to be reunited, to change form and condition, to die and to be re-born...the series of human transitions...is indeed a cosmic conception that relates the stages of human existence to those of plant and animal life and ...joins them to the great rhythms of the universe."[3] Ultimately these rituals have not only a social significance but a cosmic or ontological one.

Victor Turner, a contemporary anthropologist, has developed van Gennep's analysis of the rites of passage into an interpretive framework for social research. Turner notes that in the history of social anthropology, the dominant paradigm has been centred around the notion of social *structure*, i.e., the rules, roles and norms that govern and stabilize human interaction. Rituals have primarily been understood as having a conservative character, as confirming the dominant structure of the social group. Turner, however, goes back to van Gennep's analysis of the role of transitions in rituals.

Turner coins the term "liminality" to designate the state of being in a transitional or liminal space. Liminality is a position of structural outsiderhood and inferiority. To be liminal is to be vulnerable, without the protection of role or office. At the same time, liminality implies potency, the capacity to become more than one has been. The liminal person is "naked", as it were; he or she is without defenses yet has what Turner calls "the powers of the weak."[4]

Furthermore, liminality need not imply isolation. In the ritual process, not only the individual but others, sometimes even the whole community, pass into a liminal stage. In such a condition, they stand before each other divested of the masks emblematic of their social status. They meet not as a series of individual "I'"s but as an "essential We", a community characterized by the feeling of "humankindness". Turner calls this social condition, "communitas". The ritual process introduces communitas into the structured life of a group; it breaks down norms in order to renew and regenerate social life.

Ritual, then, is inherently *creative*, not primarily conservative, as earlier anthropologists had thought. As Turner says, "liminality, marginality and structural inferiority are conditions in which are frequently generated myths, symbols, rituals, philosophical systems and works of art."[5] Those who occupy the sacred and dangerous position of the "outsider" are free of the prevailing paradigms and can fashion themselves anew. They are capable of creating "root metaphors" or "conceptual archetypes" which can later be unpacked and serve as the basis for the formation of social structures. These metaphors or archetypes are multivocal; they bring together body and spirit in a felt and imagined unity.

Liminal creativity works through the imagination; it does not abstract from the concrete conditions of life, as does the logic which structure provides. In liminality and communitas, Turner finds the basis of art. The ritual process is an artistic process, essential for the continued vitality of social life.

The liminal state is characterized by an acceptance of pain and suffering. The vulnerability, poverty and "nakedness" of those in this condition opens them up to the limitations of the human condition, limitations which are usually masked or hidden by social structure. Turner compares liminality to tragedy, "for both imply humbling, stripping and pain".[6] In this vulnerable state, the individual is capable of receiving wisdom, a "deep knowledge' that comes from an awareness of one's limitations. Indeed the tragic hero, such as Oedipus, achieves wisdom only by entering a liminal state and encountering his or her essential suffering. This wisdom is received as a gift from the gods, the more than human powers that sustain us. Artists who are capable of embodying this tragic wisdom in a root metaphor provide a vision that can sustain their community. For without vision, it is written, the people perish.

Before returning to the theme of the presentation with which I began, I would like to develop one more set of ideas, centred around the notion of the "gift". I believe this notion is central to an understanding of how the presentation "works". In fact, I would go so far as to say that the presentation only works if it partakes of the spirit of the gift, i.e., if it is truly a "present" and not a "performance".

The gift was first described as an essential element in social life by another French sociologist of the first part of this century, Marcel Mauss. Mauss contrasted gift exchange in archaic societies with market exchange in the modern world. What characterizes gift exchange is a three-fold set of obligations: the obligations to give, to receive and to repay. The gift is not only a material thing; as Mauss says, "to give something is to give a part of oneself".[7] Gift exchange is therefore not a purely economic event, rather, it is what Mauss calls, a "total social fact", with religious, legal, moral, aesthetic and economic aspects. In order to understand the exchange of gifts, we have to take into account all the aspects of gift-exchange, not just the material or economic ones.

Most important of all for Mauss is the social nature of the gift. Because of the obligation to receive and re-pay, the giving of a gift creates a social bond between different individuals. And because the gift is also a gift of self, this bond is an intimate and familiar one. The spirit of the gift links individuals in archaic societies into a cohesive whole bound by reciprocal obligations. As Mauss says, "in giving...a man gives himself, and he does so because he owes himself — himself and his possessions — to others."[8]

Like van Gennep, Mauss aims at a disinterested objectivity in his account of gift exchange. And like van Gennep as well, Mauss is led to conclusions that go well beyond his scientific method. Although he is at pains to point out that the obligations involved in gift exchange can be onerous, he concludes by praising the ethical and social benefits of exchange based on the gift as opposed to the market exchange of our own culture. Just as gift-giving binds social agents together, so market-exchange sets them against one another. In the market, it is necessary to calculate my interest in opposition to yours; exchange pushes us further apart rather than joining us in a common bond. A society based on the market can never achieve the sentiment of sociality that is necessary for human well-being. Thus the study of the gift in archaic societies reminds us of the essential basis of social life.

Lewis Hyde, in his book, *The Gift: Imagination and the Erotic Life of Property*, has developed Mauss' ideas on gift exchange into a general theory of art. "A work of art is a gift", he says, "...a thing we do not get by our own efforts. We cannot buy it, we cannot acquire it through an act of will. It is bestowed upon us".[9] The work is a gift in three different senses or, rather, there are three phases through which the work must pass in order to become a gift.

First, the basis of the work comes to artists in an intuition or inspiration that is bestowed upon them. Artists must open themselves up to this source of inspiration; they must become "empty" or "poor" so that the material can fill their soul. But secondly, artists must use their talent, their gift, to work on the material; Hyde calls this the "labour of gratitude" which gives thanks for the gift of inspiration. Finally, artists must themselves bestow the gift on others; they express their thanks for the gift which has been given by donating it to others.

Hyde's vision of art as a gift is opposed to art as commodity. The spirit of the gift is lost when it is not given away but sold. In this respect the gift is unique among things in that it stays alive only when it is consumed. A gift that is not given but held onto or sold loses its spirit and dies. But when the gift freely circulates, it not only maintains itself but actually increases in value.

This notion of the increase involved in gift exchange is taken from Mauss' analysis of gift exchange in archaic societies, in which the obligation to re-pay a gift takes the form of an obligation to give a greater gift in exchange, thereby demonstrating one's own superior status. Hyde elaborates this notion into a broader social and aesthetic context. For him, the increase lies primarily in the bond which the gift creates. The gift is erotic, i.e., it brings together or unites diverse elements into a felt and intimate whole. The increase is first to be seen in the work of artists, who take the materials of their life, their felt experiences of objects and of other living beings, and bring them together into a coherent and living unity. Artists vivify their material by their work. The "increase" is the life which has been given to dead matter.

But secondly, the circulation of the work binds together artist and audience into a greater cultural or spiritual tradition. When we receive the gift of a genuine work of art, we ourselves enter the "gifted state" and become open to our own spirit. The gift that is contained in the work thus has the power to create a spiritual community, to "increase" a social group by bringing it to life.

We can see here how the ideas of Turner and Hyde converge. To envision art as gift is also to foresee the possibility of communitas among human beings. It is not only that communitas creates art, as Turner pointed out, but also that art creates communitas, as Hyde indicates. Wherever a work of art is given and received in an authentic manner, a community springs into being. This is why Heidegger calls art an "origin" (Ursprung); it is the original spring or leap which binds together and gives life to an historical community."[10]

Moreover, just as Turner understands liminality as central to communitas, so Hyde sees the gift of the work to be a liminal or threshold gift. Such gifts, he says, act as agents of individual transformation; they are signs of the death that is necessary so that re-birth may occur. Artists "die" each time they enter the gifted state; they must leave behind the familiar territory of what they know and own and enter the no-man's land of ignorance and poverty. It is only when they are "empty" or "dead" in this sense that they can find room for what has been given to them and come to new and regenerated life. Artists must undergo the suffering of liminality in order to receive the gift which they will give to others, thereby creating the communitas in which they can become aware of their own giftedness.

If we return now to the topic of the presentation with which we began, we can begin to understand its significance. First of all, the presentation is clearly a rite of passage; it effects a transition in the existence of the presenter from one who is "ignorant" or "outside" of the realm of expressive therapy to one who has entered this world. It is an initiation rite, in which, as van Gennep says, "the magic circle is broken for the first time, and, for that individual, it can never again be completely closed."[11] Certainly, it does not complete the transformation; it is only a beginning. But, as Heidegger indicates, a "beginning" can also be an "origin"; it can initiate a creative leap into new possibilities of development. Thus the presentation can perform the function of a rite of passage; it can lead the individual on the path to a new "territory", a new way of being oneself and being with others.

The presentation also has the structure of a rite of passage. It requires the presenter to separate him or herself from the group, to enter a liminal state of suffering and vulnerability, and finally, to be re-incorporated into the community. All three of these phases are necessary for the presentation to "work", i.e., for it to be an act of transformation. If presenters cannot detach themselves from the group and enter the liminal state, nothing will have been accomplished. But if the group cannot re-incorporate them in this changed condition, the presentation will remain incomplete and ineffectual. Thus the presentation requires the participation of the group if it is to succeed. This participation primarily takes the form of the "feedback" referred to earlier.

We can see now that the presentation as a rite of passage is essentially to be understood as an exchange of gifts. What presenters give us is, as Mauss noted to be the case with all genuine gifts, a gift of self. In this case, it is the gift of their suffering, the trauma or wound that marks their soul. This gift is offered freely to the group. In exchange, the group gives "feedback". That is, the group becomes alive to its own giftedness through the gift of the presentation, and, in gratitude, wishes to complete the circle by returning the gift. Feedback is the gift given back again with increased vigour.

It is remarkable how often the quantity and quality of the feedback is in direct proportion to the depth and intensity of the presentation. If the group is not "moved" or "touched" by the presentation, i.e., if the group has not been brought to life by it, then it cannot respond in kind but can only offer silence or a token acknowledgement that a formal obligation has been undertaken. When the gift is given freely, however, then the group often responds by heaping gifts upon the presenter, who is thus "filled" after having "emptied" him or herself through the presentation. The whole community then shares in the abundance that is created by the exchange of gifts.

Two things distinguish the presentation from other modes of gift exchange. In the first place, what is given in the presentation is the suffering of the presenter. In daily life, this suffering is often what we try hardest to keep to ourselves; we resist giving it away for fear that it will not be recognized or accepted. But, more primarily, we do not give it away because we do not "own" it; i.e., we do not accept it as that which belongs to us.

Most of us do not view our suffering as a gift to be treasured; we see it instead as a foreign object that has entered our souls and must be expelled. We repress it, deny it, project it, do anything we can to rid ourselves of it. Our suffering is what hurts us, what causes us pain; and our natural reaction is to avoid pain and seek pleasure, as Freud pointed out so clearly in his account of psychic life.

The basis of the presentation, however, is that our suffering must be viewed as a gift. In the first place, it is a gift in that it has been given to us. We "suffer" it, i.e., we undergo it through no choice of our own. In fact, we "suffer" when we can no longer choose, when we are no longer in control of our lives, when we have reached the limit of our power, our capacity to act. The Greeks knew that it is part of the human condition to experience our limits, the place where our will fails us and we are forced to confront what we lack. This knowledge is the basis of tragic art. Suffering, to the Greek poets, is a "gift" from the gods. And this was also the young Shakyamuni's experience: even the privileged existence of a prince cannot hide forever the necessity of age, illness and death.

But our suffering is also a gift in the second sense that it can be the basis of our power and vitality. When Shakyamuni discovered suffering, he abandoned the palace of his father and went in search of a remedy. In the end, all his attempts at eliminating suffering failed. It was only when he came to accept that existence *is* suffering that he achieved enlightenment and became a Buddha. That is, he had to experience suffering not as a condition extrinsic to life that could be eliminated but rather as the very core of existence. Paradoxically, this experience led him not to greater suffering but to compassion, infinite compassion for all beings, including himself. This compassion is another word for joy.

Similarly, for the tragedians, the one who "suffers" is also "blessed". The gods wound only those whom they love. The wound becomes a gift if it is accepted, if it is "borne". When Oedipus dies, the ground on which he lies becomes holy ground; he has made it sacred and a gift to others by the acceptance of his own limitations.

The presentation distinguishes itself from other forms of gift-giving in that the origin of the gift is not pleasure but pain. Nevertheless, the pain that is accepted and treasured as one's own can be a source of wisdom and joy. This is the "joyful wisdom" of which Nietzsche spoke. Only when one's suffering has been "owned", i.e., accepted with loving compassion and insight, can it be "given away", for we cannot give what we do not own.

When our suffering becomes a gift, when we have the courage to "bear" it as our own, then we can give it away to others. And the gift that we give them then is the capacity to accept and understand their own suffering. When the presenter "touches" others with his or her pain, then they are "moved" to undertake the same journey, to perform the same act of inner transformation. Often members of the group will be moved to express their own sorrow, to "testify" or "witness" to their own experience of limitation.

What is wonderful is that the exchange of suffering forms a community of healing. When the spirit of the gift touches the group, sorrow is transformed into joy. This is not the "happiness" that comes from avoiding pain, a condition that is shallow, transitory and unreal. Rather, it is the deep, abiding and authentic encounter of soul with itself and soul with other. It is communitas, the experience of humankindness.

The presentation is also distinguished from ordinary kinds of gift exchange in that the gift that is to be given is in the form of a work of art. Presenters do not merely show their suffering mutely or manifest it in the inarticulate mode of tears or a cry of pain; rather they must take this pain and find a form in which to contain it. This requires that they actively confront their suffering and enter that "gifted state" of which Hyde speaks. The suffering is not thereby diminished or eliminated; instead the containment allows them to bear it more willingly.

Art provides the container in which pain can be "borne". Without this container, the psyche cannot "hold" its suffering; the intensity is too much to bear. Art creates the form in which intensity of feeling can be contained. This form does not eliminate or decrease the pain; rather it permits intolerable sorrow to be accepted and "owned". Containment increases intensity. By making art out of suffering, the presenter acquires an "increase" over the mere undergoing of his or her fate; presentations often end with presenters experiencing a renewed sense of power and aliveness. Their "problems" are not "solved"; but the mystery which they are acquires a tragic beauty and grandeur.

In confronting what has been "dead" in themselves and bringing it to life, presenters give a gift of renewed vitality to the group as well. A bond is created between them and others which often takes the form of physical closeness and touching. A sense of communitas arises in the group as members struggle to empty themselves and receive the gift of self which the presentation brings. When this occurs, feedback is no longer an obligation but a form of thanksgiving, a spontaneous act of gratitude. As presentation follows presentation, bonds are formed within the group. The group thus has the potential to become an erotic nexus of gifted souls, a community of artist/healers.

I want to emphasize that I am talking here about the ideal case. Often the presentation does not succeed or is only partially successful. Presenters are blocked from entering the liminal state, usually out of fear and lack of trust. Sometimes the group is overwhelmed by the presentation and is not capable of completing the exchange in an adequate way. Even when the presentation is authentic and deep and the feedback matches its depth and intensity, the world of structure intervenes: class-time is over, the demands of daily life are omnipresent, the course comes to an end. The surrounding environment of the university is antagonistic to the experience of communitas. Timetables, grading, pressure to get into graduate school keep students from being together in any but the most superficial or competitive ways.

Still, what is striking is how often the presentation does work, as if it were activating an archetypal need longed for by all group members. We are all gifted, and we all long for that communion of the spirit that occurs when we are able to share our gifts. There are very few places in our lives where we can do this.

In the title of this essay, I write of "bearing gifts to the feast". It should now be clear what sort of gifts we are to bear: we need to be able to carry the suffering of our souls, to "bear" it within the form of art. Only thus will we become able to help others bear their own suffering. The presentation is only a beginning; but certainly it is an essential first step in this process. Without it, we join the legion of "helpers" everywhere, who carry their pain only on the shoulders of those whom they "help". It is ironic that helpers do not wish to burden others with their troubles and instead keep them to themselves. If they could only give these troubles away in the form of a gift, they would do more than all the brave "shouldering" in the world.

But why speak of a "feast"? Many accounts of the archetype of the wounded healer, to which this paper may be understoood to refer, emphasize the liminal state in which the healer obtains his or her power. Often however, there is not an adequate recognition of the fact that liminality is only a phase in the initiatory rite of passage that marks the education of healers and therapists. The rite is incomplete unless the novice is re-incorporated into the group; otherwise, he or she becomes a permanent "outsider" or "marginal" character. In fact, our dominant vision of the artist is of such an outsider. But artists or healers are only "outsiders" in a society in which all members are "outside" of one another. When gift exchange gives way to the market economy, the social bond deteriorates and society becomes a "war of each against all".

Certainly, anyone who enters a liminal state, who undergoes a process of spiritual death and re-birth, becomes ec-static, i.e., steps "outside" the normative world of daily life. But in traditional societies, ecstasy is only a moment in the emergence of spiritual power. In order for this power to be realized, it must be received into the group. Otherwise, it is blocked, and implodes, giving rise to an inflation of the ego and a belief that the power is the property of the individual. A gift must be consumed in order to stay alive; it must be continually given away or it will die. And for it to be given away, there must be others who are willing to receive it. This reception is the "feast" of which I am speaking.

It may be that the earliest form of human solidarity was the communion meal or feast. Certainly eating together has become a metaphor for many of our most powerful rituals. The Passover Seder of the Jews and the Last Supper of the Christians, itself a passover feast, are "root metaphors" for these spiritual communities. The Sabbath bread and wine in Judaism, transmuted into the Christian communion offering, are symbolic media through which communitas is formed.

All festivals may be seen to be related to primitive feasts, and almost all involve some form of feasting. It if is not literal food that is involved, it is the food of the spirit that all share (or in some festivals, the food of the flesh, e.g., carnival). The feast is the original form of communitas.

Moreover, the consumption of the gift is often thought of as a form of "eating". The potlatch of the Northwest coast native peoples, for example, was a big give-away, in which status was acquired by the value of that which was donated. Hyde points out that "'potlatch' means a 'feeder' or 'place to be satiated'".[12] Gifts are meant to be consumed like food; and like food, they nourish us. As food, a material thing, nourishes the body, so art, a thing of the spirit, nourishes the soul.

The "feast", then, is the event in which gifts are received and exchanged. The presentation is not complete until the "feedback" is given. Both presentation and feedback nourish the participants and give them renewed life. This "increase" of vitality itself demands to be given away. Those who have become "gifted" as expressive therapists, therefore, have the obligation to give their gifts away, to go outside the circle of the group and donate their services to others. Otherwise the group itself becomes "special" and "outside" of the wider human community. Its work can become self-indulgent and precious; ultimately the work may lose its power and become a parody of itself.

The gift must be given away if it is to stay alive. Only by being consumed or "eaten" does it generate an increase in vitality. We must continue to bear our gifts to the feast if we wish to share in the communion of renewed life which they bring. It is in this spirit that I offer this essay: as a gift for all that I have received and as a sign of my willingness to join with others in a community greater than its parts. I hope that readers will give me their feedback and that, when we have "eaten" together, we will find that there is more than when we began.

References

1. Van Gennep, Arnold, *The Rites of Passage*, Chicago, 1966, p. 11.

2. Ibid., p. 81.

3. Ibid., p. 194.

4. Turner, Victor, "Liminality and Communitas", *The Ritual Process*, Harmondsworth, Middlesex, England, 1974, p. 95.

5. Ibid., p. 116.

6. Turner, Victor, "Humility and Hierarchy", in Turner, op. cit. p. 191.

7. Mauss, Marcel, *The Gift*, New York, 1967, p. 10.

8. Ibid., p. 45.

9. Hyde, Lewis, *The Gift: Imagination and the Erotic Life of Property*, New York, 1983, p. xi.

10. Heidegger, Martin, "The Origin of the Work of Art", in *Poetry, Language, Thought*, New York, 1975. pp. 77-78.

11. Van Gennep, op. cit., p. 177.

12. Hyde, Lewis, op. cit., p. 9.

Image Abuse and the Dialectic of Interpretation

What does it mean to interpret an image in art therapy? That we raise this question at all is an indication of the confusion and conflict that exists within the field. On the one hand, there are textbooks and manuals that tell us how to interpret images according to standardized norms. On the other hand, there is a widespread reaction against "image abuse", interpretations that reduce the image to pathological structures and thereby eliminate its intrinsic content and depth. Is the image a symptom whose meaning is hidden to the patient? Or is it a symbol consciously crafted? What is the function of the therapist in the interpretation of images? Who is it that knows the meaning of the image and how is this meaning to be elucidated? As Shaun McNiff has indicated, "Art therapy has given little attention to the epistemological bases of its interpretive practices."[1] In this article I would like to examine some of these epistemological bases by reflecting on the history of interpretation in depth psychotherapy and in modern philosophy. In so doing, I hope to provide a framework that can take account of the varying modes of interpretive practice and to find a unified perspective in terms of which art therapists can see their work.

We might do well to begin by looking at interpretation in psychoanalysis. The origins of psychoanalysis lie in the treatment of hysteria. The hysteric patient suffers from symptoms whose causes are obscure. His or her symptoms are physiological and similar to those displayed by victims of neurological disease or trauma, yet there is no sign of neurological disturbance. No wonder that the hysteric was often treated as a malingerer by frustrated physicians. As long as the symptom is understood within the aetiological framework of physiological cause producing physiological effect, it remains a mystery and an irritant to science. The great discovery of Freud is not that hysteria has a psychological cause but that the hysterical symptom has a meaning. In the framework of cause and effect, the effect does not signify the cause; it merely stands as its product. There is no intrinsic meaning connection between cause and effect, one just happens to invariably follow the other. The hysterical symptom, on the other hand, has significance. It means something to the person who suffers from it. But what it means is obscure. The patient does not know the meaning of his or her symptom. In fact the meaning has been systematically distorted and hidden. The task of psychotherapy is to bring the hidden meaning into the light.

At first Freud conceived of the hidden meaning of the symptom as a memory trace that had undergone repression due to its painful affect. Traumatic emotional experiences were shut out of consciousness and buried in a split-off portion of the mind. Their energy, however, found expression in symptomatic form. By talking about the symptom and its associated memories without constraint, the patient could relive the original emotional experience and eliminate the need for symptomatic release. Psychoanalysis as a talking cure has for its goal the interpretation of the symptom and the revelation of its hidden significance in the repressed emotional experience of the patient.

For Freud, the repressed emotions seemed to centre around early sexual experiences, particularly incestuous ones. It made sense that these experiences should be so painful that they would need to be blocked from conscious awareness. Gradually, however, Freud came to doubt that many of these experiences had actually taken place. He began to believe that far from being actual memories, the incestuous scenes were in fact the product of fantasies, that each of us harbours deep incestuous desires which we need to repress in order to mature. Hysterics were not primarily atypical victims of incest; rather they suffered from a universal condition and were unique only in their inability to successfully repress or sublimate their deepest desires.

We cannot discuss here the contemporary critique of Freud's theory of hysteria, based on the discovery of the widespread prevalence of incest. What is important for our purposes is that in Freud's thinking, there is an essential connection between fantasy and desire. We never encounter desire in its raw state of libidinal energy. Rather desire always represents itself in imaginal form. The foundation of mental life is our capacity to represent our desires in the form of images. Whether dream, neurotic symptom or work of art, in each case the image is a representation of a fundamental mode of desire. We have to trace the image backwards and downwards, backwards to childhood wishes, downwards to the most primitive level of the psyche. But when we get to the bottom of the image, to its origin, what we find is another, more primitive fantasy. Interpretation does not eliminate fantasy; instead it leads us to our most essential fantasies, those that are universal to the human condition. The great discovery of Freud is that the psyche is imaginal. Interpretation makes imagination more authentic.

We can see this point of view operating in psychoanalytic practice. Free association is designed to increase the patient's access to his or her fantasy life. The method of psychoanalysis is the controlled production of imagery. By lying in a relaxed position with a minimum of external sensory cues, the patient is encouraged to fantasize. Moreover the discovery and encouragement of transference means that analysts let themselves be used as objects of fantasy. The fantasy of the identity of the analyst is the first step to the discovery of the primary fantasy objects of the patient. Here, interpretation moves from one image to another, from the superficial level of here and now imagery to the deep level of the images that lie buried in the recesses of the person's mind. When the analyst interprets the patient's fantasy about him or her as a disguised substitute for a more primary image of the patient's father or mother, he or she is using interpretation as a guide to a deep structure of fantasy that is normally inaccessible to the patient's conscious mind. He or she is not, however, eliminating fantasy altogether.

There has been a great deal of confusion about this point. The problem originates in Freud's own self-conception. As Jurgen Habermas has pointed out, there is a discrepancy between the method that Freud uses in his practice and the attempt he makes to understand what he is doing.[2] In his case studies, we can see Freud moving from one level of fantasy to another; depth psychotherapy here means leading the patient to a more fundamental level of his or her imagination. But in his metatheoretical writings Freud sees the task of psychoanalysis as the elimination of fantasy in favour of reason. "Where id is, there ego shall be", means not so much bringing my fantasies into the light as overcoming them and enabling myself to engage in a rational analysis of my situation. In these works, Freud is relying on a normative view of science in which psychoanalysis is understood as a science of mental life. From this point of view, the hysteric suffers from a disease of the imagination; it is not so much that his or her fantasies are distorted but more that they suffer from an excess of fantasy. The analyst as scientist cures by eliminating fantasy and replacing it with reason; it is a surgical procedure ending in the amputation of imagination. Interpretation here is the knife that cuts away the infected and swollen appendage. Fantasy is replaced by reality; the patient is set free to encounter the world as it is, without the distorting lens of his or her imaginative creations.

What is interesting about Freud's theory here is that the more scientific he tried to become, the more he was led to engage in the wildest forms of speculation. The primal horde, the killing of the primal father, Moses the Egyptian, Leonardo and the vulture, all these notions far transcend the empirical data of Freud's consulting room, let alone any rational approach to history and culture. Even the rock-bottom foundation of the science of psychoanalysis, the theory of instincts, turns out to be, in Freud's own admission, "mythology". Eros and Thanatos derive their explanatory power not from their cognitive status but from their function as archetypal images, personifications that are embodied in imaginative form.

Again we are struck by the ambivalence in Freud about the nature of the psyche, reflected in the ambiguous nature of interpretation in psychoanalytic theory. Insofar as the mind is a field for the production of images, interpretation serves the purpose of guiding us to the most primary and potent forms of imagination. But insofar as the mind is conceived of as rational in its essence if not its actual form, then interpretation has for its purpose the elimination of imagination, the purging of the mind's pollution by fantasy. One can see this ambivalence expressed in the history of psychoanalysis. On the one hand, psychoanalysis is conceived of as a biological science, fulfilling Freud's vision as expressed in the *Project for a Scientific Psychology*. On the other hand, psychoanalysis becomes a literary form, an imaginative mode of encountering the world and the self.

If we look at Freud's attitude to art, we can see the recurrence of his ambivalence toward the imagination. Freud was fascinated with art and artists. His collection of antiquities was a prominent feature of his consulting room. Needless to say, he was a cultured person whose writings are strewn with literary references,. In fact his references to artists, poets and novelists far outstrip his references to scientists. He gave a great deal of attention to the interpretation of works of art and published several essays on this subject. Moreover, artists and their works play a special role in Freud's understanding of the psyche. Art is seen as an alternative to neurosis. The artist is the model of the process of sublimation; he or she alone can retain the energy of the primary drives without repression. Their access to the imagination is relatively undistorted, enabling them to represent in conscious form the most deep-seated and hidden impulses of human nature. It is not an accident that Freud chose an image from literature (the Oedipus complex) for what he considered the most fundamental representation of a fantasy that for the normal individual is lost to awareness.

Yet there is a certain patronizing tone in Freud's writings about art and artists. For Freud, artists shrink from grappling directly with reality. They resort to fantasy because they are too sensitive and weak to live in the world as it is. They construct an imaginary world in order to escape an intolerable reality. Furthermore, artists know not what they do. Their creations come relatively unmediated by the conscious mind. They are blind to the significance of their own actions. Here psychoanalysts have the advantage. As interpreters of images, they can reveal the true significance of the work. They alone hold the key to the meaning of the artist's creation. The scientist's knowledge is superior to the creator's art.

Unfortunately, the analyst's interpretations are often more fantastic than the imagery contained in the work. The scientific interpretation of psychoanalysis covers up the imaginative character of interpretation. The fantasies that ensue turn out to be projections rather than deeper pathways into the object. Interpretation then becomes counter-transference, made worse by pseudo-scientific rationalizations. It is no wonder that critics of psychoanalysis turn against interpretation per se and see analysis as the enemy of art.

It seems to me, however, that such "image abuse" is by no means a direct consequence of the application of psychoanalytic interpretation. Once we recognize that drive derivatives are all we have, that there is no unmediated access to the psyche, that mental life is imaginal in its essential form, that in fact the notion of a reality without fantasy is itself an unexamined fantasy, then interpretation ceases to take the form of an assault against the image. Rather, interpretation can ben seen as the exploration of the image, the journey into the interior of the image, its central point of origination. One can speak here, following James Hillman, of "befriending" the image, of entering into a relationship with it, even of loving it.[3] Then interpretation itself becomes an erotic act. One has to love the image, become close to it, accept it on its own terms, let it speak in its own voice. It is not necessary to substitute a cognitive meaning for an image; in fact, the image will hide from all attempts to enter it cognitively. Rather, one must approach the image with imagination; one must open up a field or space for the image to show itself. This openness to the image does not mean that we rest content with the immediate appearance of the image, that we take it at face value. Freud's great discovery is that the image has depth, that staying with the image means entering into it on a deeper level, that as we stay with it, it itself leads us back to its origin.

There is then no necessary connection between psychoanalytic modes of interpretation and the attack upon imagination. On the contrary, psychoanalysis can be a means of opening up the imagination to its depth dimensions, a dimension of which it was unaware. Naturally, there is resistance to this procedure; images are buried in the psyche because they carry within them pain and suffering. The discovery of primal images is a painful process.

We come now to the problem of psychopathology. Image abuse is sometimes connected with pathologizing, the tendency to see sickness everywhere. Again, we would see this problem as tied up with the self-misunderstanding of psychoanalysis. There is a difference between seeing the imagination itself as pathological and seeing the image as a representation of my suffering. As Hillman points out, pathology is intrinsic to psyche; suffering is part of the human condition. Of course, the image expresses my pathology;

but this view only leads to image abuse if I fantasize a perspective in which suffering is eliminated. If I conceive of the conscious mind as the rational controller of a reality devoid of the imaginal, then I must conceive of the image as containing a pathology which can be eliminated. But if desire involves suffering by its very nature, then the image which expresses both the lack and the fulfillment of desire needs to be preserved and given space to show itself. This is why the most profound images in art are images of suffering: the image of Oedipus purifies the soul not de-spite his suffering but because of it. Christianity expresses this through the image of a suffering God. Psychopathol-ogy, the suffering of the soul, is what the image needs to express. Interpretation, then, to do justice to the nature of the soul, needs to attend to the pathology in the image.

Attending to the pathology in the image is different from reducing the meaning of the image to a diagnostic category. The whole notion of diagnosis has to be re-cast in imaginal form. What are the primary images of psycho-pathology? These are the categories that we mistakenly treat as purely cognitive truths. Our categories are fantasies. This does not make them untrue; rather they are true to the extent to which they are true fantasies, i.e., fantasies which express the primordial images of the suffering of the soul. This is why Oedipus can be a complex as well as a myth; we suffer from an Oedipus complex to the extent that we enter into the myth of Oedipus, to the extent that his story is our story. Changes in diagnostic categories thus imply changes in myths; Narcisssus replaces Oedipus as we un-cover the image of the self before it relates to others. Diag-nosis is essential; we need to know whose story it is that we are telling, what myth our images point to. Diagnosis only becomes pernicious when we forget that we are telling a story, when we think that our categories replace the image with rational explanations. The interpretation of the image in terms of its psychopathology, far from being an abuse of the image, can, if conducted in imaginal terms, express an attitude of awe and reverence for the suffering contained within the image, the suffering of the person's soul presented through the image.

Is psychoanalysis then an adequate framework for the interpretation of imagery in art therapy? I would answer that it is adequate to the extent to which it is itself imaginal, to the extent to which it can recognize itself in the field of the imagination and give up its pretence of belonging to a superior realm of cognition. The analyst or therapist would then be an explorer of the undiscovered country of the mind. His or her goal would be dis-covery, the uncovering of what is hidden. This hidden is not different from what is manifest; it is the deeper, more fundamental nature of what immediately appears. Interpretation goes from surface to depths, from veiled appearance to the shining-forth of the essence. But interpretation never escapes the imaginal as such. The essence is not a concept; it is a deeper image, a more fundamental representation of what is immediately encountered.

Moreover, if analytic interpretation is pursued to its limit, it transcends itself. This is what Jung and, following him, Hillman, have recognized. In the suffering lies the cure. The image that leads us backward and downward to the suffering psyche also leads us upward and forward to its healing. Oedipus' self-knowledge leads to his blindness; but his suffering itself becomes a blessing upon the land. The myth is only completed when Oedipus dies at Colonus; Thebes is but a part of his journey.

Freud's scientism and fondness for aetiological explanations have prevented psychoanalytic theory from grasping an essential feature of imaginal life; its tendency towards hope and joy, towards imaginative perfection and harmony. Here Jung's image of the self as a mandala is helpful; the psyche represents itself not only through images of suffering but also through images of salvation. There is a utopian cast to the psyche which matches its descent into the underworld. Heaven as well as Hell are contained within the imagination. The image takes us upwards to an angelic dimension as it also takes us downward to encounter our demons. Further, as Heraclitus noted, the way up and the way down are the same. The utopian fantasies of psyche in a state of perfection are the inverse of the dystopian image of a soul doomed to eternal pain. Christ on the cross leads to the image of resurrection; the dispersion of Israel has Jerusalem for its counter-fantasy.

Thus an adequate theory of interpretation would have to leave room for the sacred dimension of the image as well as for its pathology. Here the critique of image abuse is particularly appropriate. Anyone who has felt a numinous power in his or her artistic imagery only to have it reductively interpreted as nothing but a piece of pathology can testify to the pain caused by the abuse of the image. But conversely we all have experienced the joy of recognition when someone correctly names our image and recognizes it for its upward flight of the spirit.

Further, an image will often contain both pathological and sacred dimensions at the same time. After all, if demons are fallen angels, then we must be able not only to call up the demon but also to recognize its original nature. To love our demons, to hold them tenderly and embrace them, is to see in them our own angelic essence. This is nothing more than what every therapist worthy of the name does with his or her clients: to see in the distorted features of their suffering faces their original innocence and capacity for love. Can we do any less with the images they create?

For depth psychology to attend to the fullness of the image, it must supplement the psychoanalytic interpretation that goes downward and backward with a psychosynthetic one pointing forward and upward. Psychopathology must be integrated with an image of healing. The reduction to the family romance must be connected with the amplification to cosmic harmony and wholeness. We need to develop a dialectical conception of interpretation which can take account of these conflicting tendencies. Otherwise our imaginative capacity is stunted; we live either in too narrow or too broad a perspective, seeing only pathology or only health everywhere. The psyche contains both; and it contains them in an intimate unity, so that one is found only through the other.

This means that interpretation in depth psychotherapy has a transcendent dimension. That this is so should come as no surprise to anyone familiar with the history of interpretation in modern thought. The study of interpretation, or "hermeneutics" as it is more formally called, begins with the exegesis of biblical texts. Its underlying premise is that the text is a distorted expression of the word of God. The task of interpretation is to find the transcendent meaning contained within the distortions of the text. It is only in the nineteenth century that interpretation comes to be identified with demystification, with a reduction from the sacred to the profane world. Nietzsche's critique of philosophy and Marx's critique of political economy treat the text as ideology, a cover-up for baser motives. Freud's perspective on interpretation falls within this framework. At the same time, as we have indicated, his perspective tends to escape it. In fact, there is a dialectic of interpretation that ensures that one cannot stay within the reductive sphere. There are unexamined notions of harmony and wholeness that sustain any reductive critique: for Nietzsche, bodily pleasure without guilt; for Marx, social solidarity; and for Freud, the conflict-free functioning of the ego, rational autonomy. Because these notions are implicit, they can be denied. But the critique as a whole makes sense only within their terms.

The philosopher Paul Ricoeur, in his intensive re-reading of the whole of Freud's work, has demonstrated this "teleological" dimension to be a necessary part of Freud's "archaeological" search for origins.[4] More generally, Ricoeur sees the mutual implication of what he terms, respectively, the "hermeneutics of generosity" and the "hermeneutics of suspicion". To read an image or a text forward and upward, to see its transcendent dimension, requires that we take on an attitude of generosity, that we give ourselves freely to the dimension of the image that overflows our preconceptions.

Here is where awe and respect for the image are absolutely necessary. Particularly in the work of art, the image reveals its transcendent dimension. But just as the image is always more than it is, so it is also always less than it is. We can read it downward and backward; we can see its descent into the underworld, its concealed suffering and anguish. This reading requires that we assume an attitude of suspicion, that we regard the image as hiding something from us, that we wrestle with it and force it to reveal its secret. Only in the to and fro of suspicion and generosity does the double nature of the image stand revealed.

This double or dialectical nature of the image may lead us into surprising paths. Sometimes, as Freud saw, the image of the Holy Father may take us back to our paternal roots; the sacred image may conceal a profane origin. But sometimes the ordinary may be illuminated by a more-than-human dimension; the image of my father may have a transcendent dimension of which I was unaware. There is such a thing as the "repression of the sublime", as well as the more common forms of repression with which we are only too familiar. A general rule of interpretation might even be to suspect the sacred image and to generously see more in the profane one than it sees in itself. If we stand within the dialectical nature of interpretation, ready to go up or down wherever the image leads us, then we will neither abuse the image by reducing it to our demonic drives nor will we inflate it by casting it in angelic robes.

The human being stands somewhere between the demons and the angels. He or she is capable of journeying to either the heavenly or the infernal realms. In fact, interpretation is necessary precisely because we venture into worlds which speak in different languages than our own. Hermes, as both messenger of the gods and as a guide of souls in the underworld, shows the double nature of the hermeneutic enterprise. Interpretation makes it possible for us to move into other worlds; if we but follow it, the image will lead us into foreign lands where we will find treasures as well as dragons who guard them. Perhaps we will even find that the dragon is the treasure. But certainly the guide will betray us and lead us astray if we do not befriend it and treat it with respect. The art of interpretation depends upon our capacity to trust in the guiding power of the image. Whither thou goest, I will go, must be our maxim. If we abuse the image, we are sure to lose the way.

References

1. McNiff, Shaun, "The Intepretation of Art", *The Canadian Art Therapy Association Journal*, Vol. 3, No. 1, 1987.

2. Habermas, Jurgen, *Knowledge and Human Interests*, Boston, 1971.

3. Hillman, James, "An Inquiry into Image", *Spring*, pages 62-88, 1977, "Further Notes on Image", *Spring*, p.p. 152-182, 1978.

4. Ricoeur, Paul, *Freud and Philosophy*, New Haven, 1970.

The Dialectic
of Creativity

From Innocence to Experience
and Back Again

Our image of creativity often is characterized by a quality of
youthfulness. We think of the child at play, the joyful, life-
affirming spirit who sets out for new territories, explores
new worlds. We contrast this with an image of aging,
losing our creative juices, moving toward death and decay.
Often we say that creativity can keep us young. In this
paper, I would like to explore the extent to which creativity
can be specific to later stages of life. It is not just that we
can "stay" creative throughout our lives; such a notion implies that we need to retain a specifically youthful quality to
protect us against the sterility of aging. Rather, I would like
to explore the notion that creativity is a life-long process,
that there are forms of creativity that develop throughout the
life-span, so that the creativity of the adult and the older
person is specifically different from that of the child and the
youth. My hypothesis is that this development is a dialectical one, that mature creativity is capable of integrating the
opposing forces within the person in order to bring him or
her to a sense of wholeness and fulfillment. If this hypoth-

esis has any validity, then there would be implications for psychotherapy as well; any therapeutic process that takes creativity seriously would have to take account of its whole range, not just its early forms of development.

In order to comprehend the difference between youthful and older forms of creativity, I would like to begin with two contrasting images to be found in the work of the poet William Blake. In his well-known *Songs of Innocence and of Experience*, Blake presents us with a clear opposition between two ways of being. "Innocence" belongs to the child; the world of innocence is the world before evil is introduced, a life-affirming, love-affirming state. Blake writes his "happy songs" so that "every child may hear." He writes them with a "rural pen"; the images are of a verdant countryside, where the "green woods laugh," with the "voice of joy". Joy is indeed the dominant state; it is an active expression of basic life energy, life freely flowing out from itself. The figure of innocence is imagined in the form of the lamb. When Blake asks, Who made the lamb?, the answer is, a god who calls himself a lamb, one who is "meek" and "mild" and who "became a little child". Innocence is the land of the Christ-child, the God of love.

But even in innocence, the shadow of experience looms. The merry sparrow is contrasted with the sobbing robin. The chimney-sweep, the little boy lost, the little black boy, all are threatened and must be protected by angelic forces. In the *Songs of Experience*, this protection is absent. The soul has "lapsed"; Earth is in chains; the child is "reduced to misery". Instead of joy, Blake writes of a world characterized by envy, jealousy, repressed anger. In the "midnight streets" of London, Blake hears the "mind-forg'd manacles". Sorrow replaces joy; it is not innocent sorrow, but the bitter tears of a blighted life. In the midst of this decay and degeneration, one figure stands out, the "Tyger", inspiring fear and dread, "burning bright, In the forests of the night." The tiger is deliberately counter-posed to the lamb by Blake. "Did he who made the Lamb make thee?", he asks. How can we conceive of a God who contains both the gentleness of the lamb and the "deadly terrors" of the tiger, who has permitted innocence to be blighted and turned into the world of experience?

There is no reconciliation in this early work of Blake; the world of innocence and experience stand starkly counter-posed. It is only the voice of the poet, the "Ancient Bard", who can contain these contraries. The bard calls the lapsed soul back to the "break of day", the "opening morn", with "image of truth new born". What enables the poet to make this call? Blake does not say; and the feeling we are left with is that experience has not been overcome, that Blake has not yet surmounted his own internal contradictions.

I would like to turn now from poetry to psychology, from two contrasting images of innocence and experience to two theories that can be seen to be based on a similar opposition. Melanie Klein, in her account of the internal world of the child, has given us a theoretical formulation that comes close in spirit to Blake's world of experience. It is interesting that for Klein, as opposed to Blake, the child is hardly innocent; the envy and jealousy that Blake describes in his *Songs of Experience* are the core of the child's world. For Klein, the child deflects its own self-destructive impulses outward. He or she aggressively attacks the mother's breast and seeks to devour it, incorporating its goodness. This aggressiveness gives rise to a fear of retaliation, which is responded to by guilt and a desire to make reparation. The child's ability to psychically repair the damage it has done, not to be overcome by its persecutory anxieties, is the key to its further development. As Klein says, "The child's early aggression stimulated the drive to restore and to make good, to put back into his mother the good things he had robbed her of in phantasy..."[1].

For Klein, this psychological process of reparation is the key to creativity. "Fear of the death of the most loved person leads to the child's turning away from her to some extent; but at the same time it also drives him to re-create her and to find her again in whatever he undertakes... The desire to re-discover the mother of the early days, whom one has lost actually or in one's feelings, is also of the greatest importance in creative art and in the ways people enjoy and appreciate it." Here creativity is emphatically not understood as an expression of childhood innocence. It is actually only because the child is capable of feeling guilt that it can be creative, i.e., make restoration for its imaginary crimes. Creativity is, then, based on experience; it is a turning back in order to repair and restore. It is in fact a process of mourning.

Hanna Segal, a student of Klein's, has developed this notion of mourning as the basis of creativity in her books on Melanie Klein and in several articles, notably "A Psychoanalytic Contribution to Aesthetics". Once the infant is able to experience the mother as a whole person, he or she feels that attacks on her will drive her away, will result in the loss of the object. "Reparative activities are ... done partly because of concern for and guilt towards the object, and wish to restore, preserve and give it eternal life; and partly in the interest in self-preservation... The infant's longing to recreate his lost objects gives him the impulse to put together what has been torn asunder, to reconstruct what has been destroyed, to recreate and to create."[2] Mourning for and recreation of the lost object provide the basis for symbol formation: "...the object to be given up can be assimilated in the ego, by the process of loss and internal restoration....such an assimilated object becomes a symbol within the ego...symbol formation is the outcome of a loss, it is a creative work involving the pain and the whole work of mourning."[3]

Klein's theories of infantile psychic life have not been universally followed, to say the least. Critics have questioned her ability to discern the early fantasy life of the infant and to accurately describe the mechanisms of defence it employs. Nevertheless, it seems to me that the notion of creativity as mourning is a powerful one and somewhat independent of the specifics of Kleinian theory. What I would question is whether the mourning process as Klein and Segal understand it is adequate to account for the creative act by itself, whether there is something missing in Klein's theory that limits her account of creativity. George H. Pollock, in a recent article, "The Mourning Process, the Creative Process and the Creation", while citing Segal approvingly, questions whether the creative work "is only a recreation. My view is that it is a new creation deriving its energy and perhaps inspiration and direction from the past, but still a successor creation and not just a replacement creation."[4] How can mourning account for new creation? The Kleinian theory of restoration ultimately reduces all creativity to a search for the lost object. It does not enable us to see how symbol-formation can lead to anything new.

Further, it can be questioned whether mourning is primarily the work of childhood. Certainly small children are anxious and often cry when faced with the absence of their nurturing caretakers, but it requires an abnormal trauma or unusual loss to turn childhood into a period of mourning. Studies of mourning in childhood, such as those conducted by Bowlby and his associates, are noteworthy precisely because they focus on situations where mourning is necessary because the caretaker is absent or dead. In fact, in these situations, the children often "pine away"; they seem lifeless or without creative energy, primarily because so much of their psychic life is bound up with longing for the lost object.

Klein's theory of creativity as reparation is ultimately grounded on her acceptance of the death instinct as a primary component of psychic life. It is the infant's own destructiveness that is projected outward towards the object. Fear of the loss of the object is grounded in the infant's attack upon it. Infants mourn the object that they have themselves destroyed. They make reparation only because they have themselves committed the offense. It is not even clear from Klein's account how an infant can acquire the power to effectively carry through the mourning process. What do we need to have in order to be able to lose? It seems as if mourning a loss requires a coherent self to begin with; otherwise we are bereft and liable to pine away.

D. W. Winnicott has explicitly questioned the basis of Kleinian accounts of creativity. For Winnicott, it is not loss that is the basis of creativity; rather, the child must first find him or herself before they can tolerate loss. The mother/infant bond must be firmly established or else loss of the object will be experienced as loss of the self, and the child will be overwhelmed.

In Winnicott's view, creativity is not a secondary or a defensive phenomenon, rather it "belongs to being alive". There is a link between "creative living and living itself".[5] Creativity is a basic expression of being; it is the child's affirmation of his or her own existence. This affirmation must be responded to and affirmed by another in order for the child to feel that he or she is who they claim to be. The mother mirrors the child's assertion of self by responding to his or her needs. Winnicott calls this process "illusion", in the sense that by responding to the child's needs in an adequate or "good-enough" way, the mother sustains the illusion that the child has created his or her own satisfaction. The child feels a sense of his or her own value and of their ability to be. On this basis he or she can then tolerate a gradual "disillusionment", as the separation process between him or her and the mother takes place.

Winnicott's theory of creativity is often associated with his notion of the "transitional object", that which occupies the space *between* mother and child. The transitional object (thumb, blanket, teddy bear, etc.) holds the relationship in symbolic form. It is the basis for all cultural experience and all creative work. As the child separates from the mother and acquires an independent sense of selfhood, he or she can play in the symbolic space of creative action. The ability to play is a sign of psychological health. But playing and creative action in general are grounded in an earlier stage of development, before transitional objects can be used. First the basic existence of the child, his or her being in the mode of self-assertion, must be affirmed, met and responded to by another before they can begin to play and to act creatively. His or her very *being* is creative; it is this "creative living" that needs to be secure before the possibility of creative *doing* can be established. In fact, Winnicott suggests that all creative action stems from the creativity of being itself.

Winnicott's vision of childhood is certainly different from Klein's. We might, in fact, contrast the two in terms of the Blakeian opposition between innocence and experience. For Winnicott, the child is not inherently destructive; he rejects Klein's notion of the death instinct as a primary psychic element. Assertiveness, for Winnicott, is not aggression in the Kleinian sense, not a self-destructive impulse turned outward. Rather it is the primary thrust of life into the world; it is being, where being is "an expression of who I am, I am alive, I am myself".[6] And the object for Winnicott (if one can speak of the mother as "object" here) is not the object of hate, envy and jealousy; it is the other who finds me as I find myself, who welcomes my affirmation of my need by satisfying it to the best of his or her ability. It is only in pathology that the object is lost to begin with; if there has not been good-enough mothering, no sense of the value of the self can develop. And without a sense of self, the person cannot create.

Here the contrast between Winnicott and Klein becomes apparent. For Klein, creativity comes after loss. It is the attempt to repair, to make restoration and re-create the lost object, the object that the child has destroyed. For Winnicott, on the other hand, creativity is based not on what is lost but on what is found; it is an affirmation of self based on the primary relationship with another. One could say that for Klein, we can only find what we have lost; for Winnicott, we can only lose what we have found, that is, we can only mourn a loss if we have a self that can survive what we have lost. Winnicottian "innocence" thus stands in stark contrast to Kleinian "experience".

How then can these two opposing theoretical formulations be reconciled? This is not only a theoretical question but also a practical one. How can we in our own lives bring together innocence and experience, joy and sorrow, the affirmation of self and the acceptance of loss? One way of answering this question is to think of creativity as developing along the life span. Perhaps we can think of innocence as the normative state of childhood, a time of finding and expressing the developing self. This is not to say that childhood is necessarily happy or free from loss. Rather it is to emphasize that the typical losses of childhood can normally be accommodated within the child's growing sense of his or her own being and value. If there has been good-enough parenting, that is, a basic acceptance of the child's own way of being, then he or she can tolerate the pain which is part of growing up. He or she can be weaned, go to school, ultimately leave home and become an independent person.

It is only when the losses are overwhelming or when the self is too weak to sustain them that childhood becomes a period of mourning. One could say that Klein's descriptions may be accurate for cases of pathology: when the self has not been mirrored or affirmed, the child cannot accept loss, for he or she has, literally, nothing to base this acceptance on. Similarly, when the loss is too great (the death or destruction of all that is loved, as in the Holocaust), then the self may be overwhelmed and forced to turn from growing into a future to mourning a past. It makes sense that Winnicott's vision of childhood was grounded on his experience as a paediatrician with normal children; Klein's generalizations fit her case studies precisely because there is in the latter a break in the developmental path.

This is not to say that mourning itself is pathological. On the contrary, the capacity to mourn is fundamental to growth. But mourning depends on living; we need to have a sense of our own being in order to accept loss. If we can do this, then the acceptance of loss enables us to begin again, to make a new beginning out of the ashes of the old.

This kind of mourning is typically the work of adulthood and of age. Even Segal, in a postscript to her classical article on Kleinian aesthetics, states that she now sees a "difference between pre-midlife and post-midlife artistic creativity...before the midlife crisis, the artist seeks more the ideal object...past the mid-life crisis, he is more in search of the re-creation of the object..."[7]

After midlife, it is appropriate for the individual to turn back and reflect upon his or her life, to come to terms with what they have lost: loved ones, their dreams, even or especially their own youth. Erikson talks about the mid-life crisis as a tension between generativity and stagnation. We might speak about re-generation, about the necessity for persons in mid-life to mourn what they have lost and to find new wellsprings of creativity. This new beginning will sometimes be an affirmation of the old way of life and sometimes require a radical departure from it. In either case, new energies are released; it is not merely a restoration of the past.

Innocence and experience, then, can be integrated through the creative process in its developmental forms. One stage does not merely follow another; rather the ability to mourn is founded upon the affirmation of selfhood. This explains the gap in Kleinian theory; by putting mourning before the formation of the self, Klein is unable to explain how mourning can be completed and a new beginning can be achieved. A cultural illustration of this point can be seen in the Jewish prayer for the dead, the Kaddish, intrinsic to the mourning process in Judaism. The prayer does not mention death at all; rather it consists of an affirmation of the power and goodness of God, an affirmation that despite death, life is worth living. Similarly, those who have attended a traditional Irish wake know that it is as much an affirmation of life as a lament for the dead.

It is not unusual for people in mid-life to feel the need for a renewed experience of their own creativity. Often individuals will turn to art forms that they may have experi-

mented with in youth and put aside. Expressive arts therapies can be particularly useful in affirming the mature individual's need for creative being and doing. The use of the
arts in psychotherapy could be understood in such cases as
providing a symbolic medium for the integration of the
person's experience with a recovery of a sense of aliveness.
The therapist's mirroring of the client's creativity would be
the basis on which the client could come to terms with past
losses and find the strength to begin again.

* * * *

I would like at this point to give an example of this
symbolic integration from my own work as a client in therapy,
by providing an account of this type of creative process
from inception to completion. It began by my having the
following dream:

> A woman had left her home, somewhere where
> wild bears lived. Someone gave her a bear card as
> a present to make her feel better. I was wondering
> what kind of present to give her.

The dominant feeling in the dream was one of loss and
longing; the woman was far from home, longing to return.
When I wrote down my associations, I came up with these:

1) A friend with whom I had run an expressive arts therapy
group, "Creativity and the Self", for two years, had recently
left Toronto and gone to study Native American rituals in
California. While on the way, she stopped to visit a communal group on the West Coast called the "Bear tribe". She
was welcomed by this group and felt so much at home that
she almost stayed.

2) Another friend had written a popular book in which the
illustrations showed bears hugging. She had recently changed
her life style and was spending more and more time in the
country writing poetry. I believed that her therapist, whom
I had begun seeing, had supported this change.

3) My wife had been talking about how much she missed our home in Martha's Vineyard where we spent summers. She expressed some of this longing in drawings of the sea and the shore. I shared her feeling; for me the Vineyard represented both the wildness of nature and the freedom of art, for it was in the time I spent there that I felt most creative.

When I reflected on this dream and my associations to it, I could not help but see certain dominant themes, particularly one about women who were creative and either went or wanted to go to wild places to express their creativity. The bear seemed to symbolize this wild, creative spirit that had been lost and needed to be found. In Jungian terms, it seemed as if my anima, or feminine self, was longing for contact with a more primal, wild masculine energy. I wrote in my journal, "My work with my therapist is to keep in touch with the bear country in myself."

In my next therapy session, I had the following fantasy:

I saw a wounded bear who was screaming. He was hurt in the heart. I put salve in his wounds and he recovered. Then I asked him to be my companion. I asked him what he needed to do this. He replied that he needed me to salve his wounds.

The next morning I woke up and wrote this poem:

The bear is roaring
    screaming
crying

His powerful arms stretch
   up
but do not grasp

They plead

Who would not take pity
    on the wounded one,
the lost one,
    the one who cries
for his mother?

Bear, I am afraid
    of your anger

If I approach you,
    will you devour me?

Will you kill me
    for who I am not?

Slowly, I come near

I see the wound
    in the heart

Can I salve it?

My hand touches
    your heart

We are free

To me, this poem shows an attempt at symbolic integration. It echoes childhood losses, as the bear, the "wounded
one...cries for his mother". The bear seems to also represent a primitive, aggressive force which needs to be human-
ized through love. By symbolically accepting the loss and
healing the wound, the poem becomes an act of psychic
liberation.

After writing this poem, I began a series of bear poems.
Each seemed to flow naturally from the one before. The
very act of writing the poems felt like "going back to bear

country", contacting the creative energy which I had experienced as far away or dormant. One poem in particular is noteworthy for what it says about the therapeutic experience. It shows how the therapist's affirmation of the client's creativity can help him or her find the courage to affirm it for themselves.

The Loneliness of the Bear

Who will comfort him?
   He is
too great for comforting
   too large
fierce
   quarrelsome

Besides, no one knows
   he is in pain

When he roars
   we scatter

Is he not
   driving us away?

His loneliness sits
   inside him
like a thorny bush

It tears
   at his heart

The blood flows
   unseen

Who will witness
   his pain?

Only a watcher
  who has conquered fear

Only a stalwart one
  who says,

"Bear, I am here
  with you

I sense your anguish

My heart too
  is torn
inside

I am with you
  heart to heart

I will not run
  from you
in fear"

When the bear hears this
  he stops his cries

He grows still
  calm

His energy
  comes back
within

His heart
  is on fire

He can run
  he can climb
he can sing

The bear sings
    a song
of remembrance

"Once I was young
    and unafraid
of myself

Once I saw
    in others' eyes
the image of
    my soul

I was beautiful
    when I looked
at my friends

Now I see no one

I am afraid
    to regard
my own loneliness

I roar in pain
    and do not
comfort myself

You who see me
    do not make me
less alone

But I can bear
    myself
better now

I can carry
    my weight
in the world

I am who I am
            and no one else
can be me"

The bear stands

            in the clearing

He lifts his head
            and sings

In this poem, the role of the therapist is made clear: she is the "watcher", the "stalwart one" who is not afraid of the bear's rage, who senses his anguish because she knows as well as he what it means to have a broken heart. She is with him "heart to heart"; she will not run from him in fear. Her presence calms the bear, restores to him his creative energy and enables him to sing his "song of remembrance". The poem is itself the song of remembrance which it names.

What is fascinating to me is that when I wrote the poem, I had no idea it was about the therapeutic process. The "you" who the bear addresses I felt to be a part of myself, the same part that salved the bear's wounds in the first poem. It was only in reading the poem afterward that I realized immediately that the watcher was also the therapist, that it was her ability to be with me in my woundedness that enabled me to find the strength to sing.

In reflecting on this process, I can see the dialectical character of the creative act. Certainly the image of the bear in the poem is an expression of the powerful force of life, an "expression of who I am, I am alive, I am myself", that Winnicott speaks of so eloquently.

At the same time, the poem is an act of mourning, of acknowledging and letting go of loss, as the bear experiences his woundedness, his aloneness, his pain. The mourning process is carried through by binding the potentially destructive aggressive energy of the bear with the healing power of love, both love from the self and love from the other. Without love, the bear's self-assertiveness becomes a destructive force, whether exercised on himself or another. The culmination of the process comes in the ability to create; the bear can "sing". His unheard cries are given voice in the poem. Thus the poem, a symbolic expression of life, holds together both primary life energy, "innocence", and the pain of loss, "experience". Blake's contrarieties find reconciliation in the poetic act.

Blake himself moved toward integration of the realms of innocence and experience in his later writings. In the prophetic works, *Milton* and *Jerusalem,* Blake envisions a new world where, as one of his commentators puts it, there is a "...restoration of Innocence to life by art". In visioning this world, "The questioning of Blake's most famous lyric has been reversed and answered - he who made the tiger also made the lamb. The new Jerusalem...will preserve the tender beauties of the old Eden".[8] In the first of these poems, it is through the poet Milton's return to Earth as the "artist-Christ" that the new Jerusalem will be built. One might say that the poet Blake builds his own symbolic Jerusalem by returning to the world of experience and finding a renewed sense of innocence. Here Blake fulfills the promise of his youth, that the "ancient bard" would call the lapsed soul to "Turn away no more". Instead of the unresolved opposition between innocence and experience, an opposition which might lead one to flee from adult life to take refuge in fantasies of a care-free childhood, Blake vows to enter the world just as it is, to build the new world and the new self in the midst of the old:

> I will not cease from Mental Fight,
> Nor shall my Sword sleep in my hand:
> Till we have built Jerusalem,
> In Englands green and pleasant land.

Blake concludes by wishing, "Would to God that all the Lords people were Prophets." We might amend his wish to read, "Would to God that all the Lords people were Poets." The dialectic of creativity from innocence to experience and back again requires of us that we descend as poets, as artists, into the lives that we have led, that we recognize and accept our experience of loss and find again the innocence that will restore us to ourselves and enable us to create our world anew.

References:

1. Klein, M. and Riviere, J., *Love, Hate and Reparation*, New York, 1964, p. 43.

2. Segal, H., *Introduction to the Work of Melanie Klein*, London, 1975, p. 75.

3. Segal, H., "A Psychoanalytic Approach to Aesthetics", *International Journal of Psychoanalysis*, 33: 196-207, 1952.

4. Pollock, N., "The Mourning Process, the Creative Process and the Creation", in *The Problem of Loss and Mourning*, ed. D. Dietrich and P. Shabad, Madison, 1990, p. 34.

5. Winnicott, D. W.,*Playing and Reality*, Harmondsworth , 1971, p. 81.

6. Ibid., p. 66.

7. Segal, H., *The Work of Hanna Segal*, New York, 1981.

8. Hagstrum, J., *William Blake: Poet and Painter*, Chicago, 1978, p. 43.

The Myth of Orpheus

Poetry as a Healing Art

Why myth? Why Orpheus? Before beginning an exploration of this particular myth, I would like to lay the groundwork for what I would call, following James Hillman, an "archetypal" approach to expressive arts therapy.[1] Hillman distinguishes between "the language of psychology and the speech of the soul." That is to say, psychology, in its attempt to develop a scientific understanding of mental life, uses concepts that are clear and distinct, as Descartes said all understanding must be in order to claim the status of scientific knowing. But the object of psychological research, the human psyche or soul, is not clear and articulated in its inner constitution. The soul is characterized by depth rather than clarity. Clarity is a phenomenon of the surface, of sight. It requires light or, in this case, consciousness. But the soul is obscure to us; it is hidden, dark. What we see of it, we see as through a glass darkly. The soul is what is unknown, unconscious. It cannot be grasped directly through clear and distinct ideas.

Instead the soul communicates itself to us indirectly, through image and myth. Whether in dreams, fantasy or work of art, the soul always presents itself through a concrete content, not abstractly. This content is like a messenger from a foreign country; the message is in a language which is strange to us. We always need therefore to interpret the messages of the soul.

Interpretation is a different mode of knowing than scientific understanding. An image or a myth is subject to multiple interpretations; no one interpretation can lay claim to absolute validity. Further, an interpretation is always relative to the situation of the interpreter. It is the meaning for me, not the meaning per se. Thus the "speech of the soul" can never be made into an objective system; it constantly demands of us that we examine it anew from our own perspective.

If this is true of psychology in general, how much more so then of expressive arts therapy. The latter requires an understanding that is particularly sensitive to image and myth, for these are indeed the language of the arts. The arts do not communicate through concepts but through images and stories, concrete content which points beyond itself and requires interpretation to be understood. Expressive arts therapy rests on the premise that imagination is the healer, that encouraging the soul to speak in its own way transforms darkness into light, the hidden and concealed into the open, and thus provides insight and release.

A theory of expressive arts therapy, then, must rest on a psychology of the imagination, a psychology that can account for this power of the imagination to care for or cure the suffering of the soul, its psychopathology. And this psychology must itself be imaginal, that is, it must be capable of imagining the psyche, of finding and interpreting the images and myths which can let psyche speak. Otherwise the soul is imprisoned in the conceptual network of psychological systems; it languishes, flees or dies. We then have that supreme irony, a psychology without the soul. Sometimes, it seems, we even have a psychology that is bent on extinguishing the soul, a psychocidal psychology.

If psychology is itself a product of the psyche, as all cultural phenomena are, would not a scientific psychology be a form of suicide? We might then ask, whence comes this rage against the soul? Is it based on the refusal to admit the knowledge that pathology is intrinsic to soul, that suffering is part of life? A culture bent on abolishing suffering will end by destroying its own basis in the human psyche.

But why Orpheus? Why this particular myth? I am particularly concerned to understand poetry as a speech of the soul, as one of the ways that the psyche reveals itself. The question as to whether poetry is a privileged way, as Heidegger, for example, suggests, cannot detain us here.[2] This question depends upon an understanding of language in relation to other modalities of the arts and, ultimately, upon the place of language in human existence. But certainly poetry is one essential way for the soul to speak. What kind of psychological understanding can grasp this form? Within the framework of an archetypal psychology outlined above, we would need to find an image and a myth that can contain the poetic. The myth of Orpheus seems to me to be one such container.[3]

In Greek mythology, Orpheus is said to be the first poet. He was given the gift of song by his father, Apollo. Orpheus' lyre is the concrete image that expresses this gift. With it, the poet can sing so sweetly that even the wild beasts are tamed. They gather at his feet to hear him. Even the rocks soften and trees bend to his song. All nature becomes silent so that Orpheus may sing. One aspect of the myth of Orpheus is, then, this pure outpouring of song, the lyric gift that sings the joy of natural being, of life.

But there is, of course, a dark side to the story of Orpheus. He marries Eurydice; but soon after the marriage she dies, having been bitten by a snake in an attempt to flee the unwanted advances of a shepherd, Aristeus. Orpheus' lyre now becomes an instrument to express his grief, as he mourns his beautiful and virtuous bride. Spurred by his longing, Orpheus descends into Hades, the land of shades, to seek his love. Before the throne of Pluto and Proserpine, he sings so tenderly of his loss that even the Furies are said to have been moved to tears. The gods relent and grant him Eurydice, on condition that he not look back on their journey up from the underworld. But Orpheus cannot resist; he must be sure that Eurydice is following him, and as he turns to look, loses her once more.

Now Orpheus is truly bereft. He knows there is no possibility of recovery. His song becomes a lament. He vows to live in solitude, a testimony to the depth of his bond with Eurydice. The women of Thrace, among whom he lives, ask for his love but are spurned. They swear revenge and hurl both spears and stones at him; but the power of his music softens these so that they land harmlessly at his feet. Then the Thracian women begin to howl, to beat on drums and blow flutes and trumpets so loudly that Orpheus' music is drowned out, "Until at last the unhearing stones reddened with poet's blood".[4]

Then Orpheus is torn limb from limb. His head and his lyre are thrown into the river Hebrus, "down which they floated, murmuring sad music, to which the shores responded a plaintive symphony". The fragments of his body are gathered up by the Muses and put into a grave, above which the nightingale is said to sing more sweetly than anywhere else in Greece. His lyre is placed among the stars. And Orpheus himself rejoins Eurydice in the land of shades, where he looks upon her once more, without fear of loss.

The myth of Orpheus exerted a powerful hold upon the Greek imagination. His capacity for renunciation was celebrated in rituals of purification or *catharsis*. These rituals invoked Orpheus not only as poet but as priest, physician and seer. In the Orphic religion, we see a unity of poetry, music and healing that presages the development of expressive arts therapies today.

The poet who most embodies the spirit of Orpheus in contemporary literature is Rainer Maria Rilke. Rilke's work can be seen as an attempt to penetrate into the very soul of poetry, to find a poetic voice purified of everything non-essential, to become the place where the poetic essence can burst into song. To achieve this purity, for Rilke, required renunciation and solitude, similar to that of Orpheus after the loss of Eurydice. Rilke's life was torn between powerful erotic urges and the need to be alone with his soul. It was during one of these periods of deliberate aloneness that the famous *Sonnets to Orpheus* were written.

These sonnets reached Rilke as a pure inspiration: "I could do nothing but surrender, purely and obediently, to the dictation of this inner impulse". [5] Within the space of one month, February, 1921, all sixty-four sonnets appeared. As Stephen Mitchell, Rilke's translator, says, "The whole experience seems to have taken place at an archaic level of consciousness, where the poet is literally the god's or the Muse's scribe".[6] Of course, this inspiration would have been impossible had not Rilke been prepared for it; in a sense, all his life had been a preparation for this work and its companion piece, the *Duino Elegies*. Nevertheless, what strikes the reader as well as the author is this sense of pure dictation, as if the poems were not only about Orpheus but were written by the first poet himself.

The sub-title of the Sonnets reads, "Written as a grave monument for Vera Ouckama Knoop". Vera Knoop was the nineteen year-old daughter of Dutch friends of Rilke's. She had been a dancer whose grace and beauty remained in Rilke's memory after her untimely death. The task of the Sonnets is the one that occupied Rilke all his life: how to include death within the sphere of life, how to accept the intrinsic necessity of death and suffering for life without giving oneself over to despair. In Rilke's own terms, the task of the poet is to bring together "praise" and "lament": to praise the very life that includes death within it as its ineluctable end:

In the words of the seventh Sonnet,

> Praising is what matters! He was summoned for that,
> and came to us like the ore from a stone's
> silence. His mortal heart presses out
> a deathless, inexhaustible wine.

> Whenever he feels the god's paradigm grip
> his throat, the voice does not die in his mouth.
> All becomes vineyard, all becomes grape,
> ripened on the hills of his sensuous South.

> Neither decay in the sepulcher of kings
> nor any shadow fallen from the gods
> can ever detract from his glorious praising.

> For he is a herald who is with us always,
> holding far into the doors of the dead
> a bowl with ripe fruit worthy of praise.

Or as Sonnet number eight begins, "Only in the realm of Praising should Lament/walk...".

Orpheus is the one who can bind together praise and lament because he has descended into the realm of the dead. "Only he whose bright lyre/has sounded in shadows/ may, looking onward, restore his infinite praise". Moreover, he has learned to die unto life, to bring his lamentation into the world of the living. The poet keeps the memory of Vera/Eurydice alive while praising the earth that bore her, the earth that "bestows".

For Rilke, Orpheus is the poet of two worlds, the world of the living and the world of the dead. "Is he someone who dwells in this *single* world? No:/both realms are the source of his earthly power". Although we cannot think their unity, cannot conceptually comprehend how such opposites can be conjoined, Orpheus brings them together in his song. The "singing god" is "a herald who is with us always,/ holding far into the doors of the dead/a bowl with ripe fruit worthy of praise".

How can we become like Orpheus, we whose minds are "split"? Not through desire, says the poet, not through the "passionate music" which must end. Rather, "True singing is a different breath, about/nothing. A gust inside the god. A wind". Rilke seems to be saying that only if we give up everything, let go of all attachment, can we live in that place of pure presence where all life is precious and all can be praised, even loss itself. In the concluding lines of the last sonnet,

> Move through transformation, out and in.
> What is the deepest loss that you have suffered?
> If drinking is bitter, change yourself to wine.
>
> In this immeasurable darkness, be the power
> that rounds your senses in their magic ring,
> the sense of their mysterious encounter.
>
> And if the earthly no longer knows your name,
> whisper to the silent earth: I'm flowing.
> To the flashing water say: I am.

This "I am" which, as Mitchell reminds us, is also the name of God, is a triumphant affirmation of life, an affirmation that comes through the transformation of loss. This is healing through acceptance, lament turned into praise. Perhaps this is the goal of all therapeutic work, to take the deepest loss that we have suffered, to abide in the immeasurable darkness, and yet to be the power that binds our senses, to continue to flow and be, when our very names have been forgotten. To say a "Yes" to all of life, even to loss and death.

Rilke uses the myth of Orpheus as a means to encounter life's deepest mysteries. His poetry is "soul-making", in Hillman's sense: it gives a depth to life that eludes all problem-solving or attempts at denial. The *Sonnets to Orpheus* are healing for Rilke and for us, insofar as they accept the pain and loss in life and transform them through art. In this respect, they are a model for therapeutic work in the arts.

* * * *

In my own poetry, the myth of Orpheus has touched me deeply. I too have lived that conflict between life and art that Rilke knew so well. Contrary impulses have assailed me, pulling me equally strongly towards love and towards solitude. I know the pain of Orpheus, who, in solitude, laments the loss of love. And, like Rilke, I long to put together the two worlds, the spirit-world of the poet and the sensuous world of the man.

The following poem was produced in a state of inspiration similar to that which Rilke describes. What is interesting to me is that the poem describes the state of mind of the poet previous to the god's appearance and after his departure as well as providing an account of his actual presence. The poem can thus serve as a description of the process of inspiration as well as provide an example of a product of that state.

The title, which came after the poem itself, expresses this process directly:

The god Orpheus makes his appearance transporting the poet to a state of ecstasy then departs leaving him alone

> To enter the place of silence
> where the words arise
>
> To choose to live in that world
>
> "Holy one of blessing
> Thy presence fills creation
> making us holy and urging us
> to live in the world of silence
> where you speak to us most directly
>
> The graveyard of the soul
> where the lilies of speech
> bloom silently like a cry"

But there is something false here
something hieratic
as though we were initiates
in the cult of verse

I resist absorption into the One
I want to taste the world

Let me build a bridge
from there to here
Let me find a way back
and live a double life

Alive and dead
in silence speaking
Let me touch the others
with my singing

For we cannot live in that world
cannot stay in deepest space

We come hurtling back
blazing
falling
landing on the earth

This earth our grave
and the soil of our becoming
our words earth-borne
carried by a breath of wind

Burned by a living sun
we taste our being in our mouths
touching tongues
our sexual bodily being
our flesh

Let the spirit world
come into passion
let the space of stillness
move us through our lives

Let us dance and sing
and praise the god beyond

who we knew once
and who remains our friend

This caress
is his message from the void:

"Be still
be patient
feel the throbbing pulse
of love

Joy is on this side of life
joy is this tenderness
the child's lips open
without fear

Open to life, my friends
open and let your heart
sing of my silent hour

Your time is now
mine eternity
live your time joyfully
let eternity abide without you

Soon you will be gathered up in me
but now live the fullness
of your time

I would like you to live always
with mouths open to life
hungry for the warm wetness
of love"

And now he is gone
suddenly as he appeared
there is pressure and darkness
the silence presses on me
I want to run
scream

Deserted
this emptiness
cruelty

I sink back and say yes
I can bear it
can wait again for
his coming

I lie
desolate
nothing happens
unbearable
screaming
unheard

And this is bitter
bitter in the mouth
that lay open

Cruel lover
will you come again
to heal me?
Are you a demon
to abandon me so?

I am calm
patient
accepting your way

Transported
aflame
bereft

I say a soft yes to you

I rest

I am relieved
I am empty of your words
I am done

Looking at the poem in terms of the process of the creative act, we see the poet beginning with an invocation to the god; he wishes to enter the "world of silence where you speak to us most directly". He likens this to a "grave-yard of the soul"; he must die in order to enter it. But almost immediately the poet resists this impulse; it seems to him to be false, pretentious, as if he could deny his earthly being. Instead he seeks to build a bridge between the two worlds, to "live a double life" of spirit and flesh. He praises the god beyond in dance and song. In response the god appears. His message, which is experienced like a caress, instructs the poet to live his life in the "fullness" of his time, open to life and to love. When the god departs, the poet is bereft; he struggles to accept his absence and expresses this loss directly. Finally he rests, understanding that absence is a necessary part of the process of creation. To be transported into another realm, to be aflame with inspiration, to feel the loss and emptiness when that inspiration is gone: all are essential moments of poetic creation. The poet is calm, able to wait until the moment when the god will come again.

On re-reading the poem, I am struck by the disavowal of the theme of renunciation, which Rilke, following the myth, stressed so strongly. Unlike Rilke's Orpheus, the Orpheus of this poem counsels staying on this side of life, letting "eternity abide" without us. Orpheus wants us to live "with mouths open to life/hungry for the warm wetness of love". And yet the poem acknowledges Orpheus' realm, the world of silence and of death; we must enter this world in order to contact the god. The poem seems to be saying that the silence and the solitude necessary for poetic creation prepare a space in which greater contact with life may occur.

In the myth, we remember that Orpheus is torn apart by the Thracian women after he refuses their invitation to love. Is the tale telling us to imitate this refusal or is it rather warning us about the consequences of such an act? Perhaps it can be interpreted either way. Such possibility of multiple interpretations illustrates the fecundity of myth. The Thracian women in the myth are, of course, devotees of Dionysus. Their fury is the voice of the god of the earth, of love, of the body, against the spirit world to which Orpheus holds true. I am reminded again of Nietzsche's distinction between the Apollonian and the Dionysian, between the god of order, measure and the individual, and the god of frenzy, sexuality and communal celebration. Nietzsche's genius was in seeing the necessity for joining the two; in his view the greatness of tragic art is its ability to combine the Apollonian perfection of poetic language with the Dionysian energy of music and dance. For Nietzsche, Greek tragedy is the *Gesamtkunstwerk* which Wagner sought to recreate in opera; tragedy holds both worlds together in dynamic tension.

Orpheus, so the myth tells us, is the son of Apollo. As W.K.C. Guthrie tells us, "The music of Orpheus, like Apollo's, is the calm, soothing note of the lyre. He has nothing to do with the wild din of Phrygian flutes and cymbals".[7] The story of Orpheus expresses the ideals of the Apollonian world, with its emphasis on spirituality, purity and renunciation. Yet Orpheus' refusal to serve Dionysus leads to his destruction.

In the development of Orphism as a religion, the Apollonian idea of *catharsis* or ritual purity is joined with Dionysian ecstasy and enthusiasm. Guthrie points out that, "The fusion would have been unnatural and difficult were it not that...*ekstasis* in one of its forms was already at home among the servants of Apollo."[8] The ecstasy of Orpheus is the ecstasy of the spirit; by itself it leads to renunciation and death to the things of the world. On the other hand, the ecstasy of Dionysus is the ecstasy of the body; by itself it leads to orgiastic frenzy and a forgetting of the spiritual side of human existence. The poet is, as Rilke says, the one who binds these two worlds together: "both realms are the source of his earthly power". Lacking this power, our minds are "split", we suffer from this diremption. But if we can, like a god, "enter through the lyre's strings", then we will know that "song is reality", that all being cries out to be transformed into art. Poetic expression binds together spirit and body in the speech of the soul.

The myth of Orpheus is an archetypal tale for understanding poetry as a healing art. It shows us how the poetic act can heal our split minds. But the capacity of the myth for multiple interpretation reveals that there are other modes of healing as well and other gods whose stories must be told. Music, dance and ritual enactment derive their power from the Dionysian spirit. For a theory of expressive arts therapy, we need to honour Dionysus as well as Orpheus. Perhaps in bringing them together, we can also bring together the different parts of ourselves.

When we recall the myth of Orpheus, let us also recall Dionysus as well. There are many gods, and their stories all can bring us messages that are healing for our souls, "healing fictions", in Hillman's words. [9] Perhaps there is no one master myth, no one story that can serve as an archetype for the creative act. And each story is subject to many interpretations; each brings a message that only the one who receives it can know. The myth of Orpheus is one such story; I have told it in the way that it was given to me: through the words of the god himself. Those who wish to know if it is true for them must listen to their own god, the power that enables them to create. Perhaps in telling each other our stories, we will bring these powers together as well. Then the speech of our individual souls will join together and make a communal hymn of praise.

References

1. Hillman, J., *Archetypal Psychology*, Dallas, 1983.

2. Heidegger, M., *Poetry, Language, Thought*, New York, 1971, p. 73.

3. Cf. Shaun McNiff, *The Arts and Psychotherapy*, Springfield, 1981, pp. 132-133.

4. Ovid, *Metamorphoses*, xi, 15 pp., quoted in; Rainer Maria Rilke, *The Sonnets to Orpheus*, trans. by Stephen Mitchell, New York, 1985, p. 172.

5. Ibid., p. 335.

6. Ibid., p. 8.

7. Guthrie, W.K.C., *The Greeks and Their Gods*, Boston, 1961, p. 315.

8. Ibid, p. 318.

9, Hillman, J., *Healing Fiction*, Barrytown, N.Y., 1983.

"AND YET"

— Poetry After Auschwitz

There can be no poetry after Auschwitz, Theodor Adorno once wrote. The statement itself is ambiguous. Does it mean there can be no poetry, no art, *concerning* Auschwitz? That the phenomenon of the concentration camps and the genocide of a people surpass the capacity of art to contain experience? That here at last is the exception to the human power to master life by endowing it with significant form?

Or does Adorno's phrase mean something even more radical, namely that Auschwitz and its concordant phenomena reveal to us the truth about humanity: the depth of suffering contained in human life and the fundamental inability of art to redeem that suffering, to save or heal us? In that case, not only would we be enjoined against making art out of the ashes of the crematoria, we would have to give up the creative enterprise altogether and admit that it was only another idle dream, another fantasy of salvation to cover up the grim reality of our fate.

These questions are particularly important for anyone concerned with the therapeutic power of the arts. Expressive therapists operate on the assumption that art can heal, that the pain and suffering of a human soul can find a form in which it can be held, and that in this experience of holding or containing, the individual can become "free" from his or her suffering. Is this belief an illusion? Does the therapist only distract or palliate the client through art? What kind of suffering *can* be contained in art, and what is the nature of such a containment? The vocation of expressive therapy is called into question by a serious encounter with the Holocaust such as Adorno suggests. We cannot proceed in a naive and cheerful manner, as if to say, "Take this, and in the morning you will feel much better", or "Make art and your troubles will fly away". Perhaps reflection on Auschwitz is necessary for us to continue with our work in full awareness.

Let us look at the two interpretations in question successively. With regard to the first, that there can be no poetry *about* the Holocaust, what is immediately striking is the vast amount of literature and art that has come directly out of the experience of the death camps. First the survivors themselves returned, like Ishmael in *Moby Dick,* to tell all, to bear witness to their fate. But soon after, a second generation of writers, artists and filmakers arose who were not themselves in the camps but who attempted to participate in them imaginatively. All these efforts, of both the first and the second generations, do not disprove Adorno directly. Indeed one could argue that Holocaust literature and art is a mistake, a failure, that this ceaseless outpouring of material demonstrates precisely the futility of the project as a whole. One could even say that the real events are in danger of being buried under our images of them. Do we see Auschwitz or do we see "Auschwitz", a representation which seduces us away from what we need to view?

The first reaction of both the survivors and of those who heard their reports was in fact a stunned silence. Could this horror be true? And what response might be adequate to its enormity? Many, like George Steiner, argued that language could not express the intensity of such suffering, that in the face of such total barbarism, the humanism of literature would only lend an aesthetic aura to what was beyond or beneath culture. The only appropriate response, then, would be a mute witnessing, an awe-filled silence that would testify to the exclusion of these events from the human realm.

Others, like Aharon Appelfeld, have written about the Holocaust only indirectly, by telling tales of the survivors' lives before or after the events themselves. Thus a certain silence is preserved. As Appelfeld has said:

> ...artistically, it is impossible to deal with it directly. It's like the sun. You cannot look at the sun; the temperature is too high. The Holocaust is a kind of temperature you cannot speak, you cannot utter, you cannot feel. You have to degradate it to an extent in order to speak of it...The unspeakable is a secret. You can only surround it. You cannot speak about it. It is like death.[1]

However, the initial silence of the survivors gave rise to a danger: that of forgetting. Perhaps those who were there would always remember, but what of the others? Would not silence enable them to avert their eyes? Elie Wiesel tells us:

> I, too kept silent for ten years. Then I felt it was not enough. But what I have tried to do is not to replace silence with words, but to add silence to the words, to surround words with silence.[2]

If there is no silence surrounding the words, they can be taken up and exchanged like the common coinage of any conversation; they become part of the chatter of *Das Man,* the "they" (if we may dare to invoke Heidegger here). Dead words, inauthentic words, words that do not strike fear and trembling into the heart but produce only a *frisson,* a little shiver of pleasure mixed with pain. Ultimately, pornography: e.g., films like *Ilse: She-Wolf of the SS.* How can the Holocaust be prevented from becoming part of the entertainment industry and its insatiable thirst for thrills?

Saul Friedlander, in his *Reflections of Nazism* accuses contemporary artists of doing just that. The second generation's attempt to re-create the Nazi epoch, in the work of Syberberg, Tournier, Fassbinder, even Steiner himself, has produced, according to Friedlander, an art that itself stirs up Fascistic tendencies in its audience: a fascination with the uneasy combination of kitsch and death, harmony and terror, that dominated the Nazi mentality. By directly reproducing its underlying spirit, these works turn Nazism into an aesthetic phenomenon. Fascination and aesthetic distance combine to produce an exorcism of the past which relieves us of our responsibility at the same time as we congratulate ourselves for finally being able to face the truth directly. Once again, Friedlander questions our capacity to speak about the unspeakable:

> the issue is one of indiscriminate word and image overload on topics that call for so much restraint, hesitation, groping, on events we are so far from understanding...The endless stream of words and images becomes an ever more effective screen hiding the past, when the only open avenue may well be that of quietness, simplicity, of the constant presence of the unsaid, of the constant temptation of silence.[3]

Notice that silence is spoken of here as a temptation rather than a solution. Ultimately, something must be said; but we must beware, Friedlander thinks, of speaking about the demonic in the voice of the demon himself. Only through quietness, humility and restraint can such matters be appropriately discussed.

Wiesel would go even further: "The only language (adequate to the Holocaust) may be a mystical language, and that language is a language shrouded in silence".[4] Whence this author's fascination for Hasidic culture, for a God who can only be approached through story and myth. Wiesel's own work shows the difficulty of making "poetry after Auschwitz". In his great trilogy, *Night/Dawn/Day,* it is only *Night,* a memoir in fictional form, that has the power to move us. *Night* is the direct testimony of the survivor, made more terrible by his age of fifteen years. By focusing on the author's relationship with his father, a bond that ultimately cannot stand against the destructive power of life in the camps, the book shows us a man in extremis. There is literally nothing for Wiesel to hold on to; the most intimate tie of love is powerless against such evil. In the end, the author, liberated from Buchenwald, sees himself in the mirror for the first time since leaving the ghetto: "From the depths of the mirror, a corpse gazed back at me. The look in his eyes, as they stared into mine, has never left me."[5] He has become a dead man, one of those who experiences life in death.

And yet,- as Wiesel says, "that is my favorite expression, 'and yet'" - and yet this dead man has gone on to write voluminously about his life, to make poetry after Auschwitz. "I must tell you the truth...I know it is impossible to do and yet I must do it".[6] Even in *Night,* there is testimony to the power of art when, in the camp at Gleiwitz, after a murderous march in the snow as the Nazis retreated from the advancing Soviet army, the prisoners, exhausted, starving, crushed against one another in a tiny barracks, unable to breath, suddenly:

> ...I heard the sound of a violin. The sound of a violin, in this dark shed, where the dead were heaped upon the living. What madman could be playing a violin here, at the brink of his own grave? Or was it really a hallucination?
>
> It must have been Juliek.
>
> He played a fragment from Beethoven's concerto. I had never heard sounds so pure. In such a silence.
>
> How had he managed to free himself? To draw his body from under mine without being aware of it?
>
> It was pitch dark. I could hear only the violin, and

it was as though Juliek's soul were the bow. He was playing his life. The whole of his life was gliding on the strings - his lost hopes, his charred past, his extinguished future. He played as he would never play again.

I shall never forget Juliek. How could I forget that concert, given to the audience of dying and dead men! To this day, whenever I hear Beethoven played my eyes close and out of the dark rises the sad, pale face of my Polish friend, as he said farewell on his violin to an audience of dying men.

I do not know for how long he played. I was overcome by sleep. When I awoke, in the daylight, I could see Juliek, opposite me, slumped over dead. Near him lay his violin, smashed, trampled, a strange overwhelming little corpse.[7]

Earlier in the book, we had been told that Juliek was one of the musicians at Buna who played military music as the prisoners marched out of the camp to do their forced labour. As Jews, the music of Beethoven was forbidden to them.

Can we speak about this incident at all? Facing the description of Juliek's death, interpretation seems presumptuous. In particular, to speak of the redemptive power of art would be a sacrilege. Juliek was not saved by his art; nor was the young boy, Elie Wiesel. And yet. And yet Wiesel's testimony does give us hope:

I try to find reason to be hopeful. It is not easy, not in the present, and yet - that is my favourite expression, 'and yet' - there is despair, and yet, on the other hand, there is joy, and yet. Nothing is complete, nothing is whole. In a strange way, I believe that, due to the despair, hope is possible, if we face our despair honestly.[8]

Poetry, then, for Wiesel, is a way of facing our despair honestly.

This brings us to the second possible meaning of Adorno's words: so much despair was uncovered at Auschwitz that not only must it not be turned into art; but also the whole enterprise of art is revealed to be an evasion, a ruse, or, in Freud's term, a defense. A defense against what? Against the horror of life itself.

Perhaps Adorno is Nietzsche's acolyte here. After the apotheosis of art in *The Birth of Tragedy,* Nietsche looked even further into himself and saw that art too was another veil in front of the abyss. The will to power is measured by how little illusion we need. Not only Platonic metaphysics and Christian morality but the whole artistic project can be seen to be *"Schein",* appearance, an illusion that tries to protect us from direct encounter with Being, with life. Thus Marcuse speaks about the "affirmative" character of culture. Art cannot but make the phenomenon "shine"; it casts the radiance of the beautiful over its subject matter and grants us always *"une promesse de bonheur".* But Auschwitz has shown us the abyss we only imagined before; in front of such horror, the imagination stands revealed as impotence, wish-fulfillment, dream or neurosis.

Furthermore, what good is art if the Nazis themselves were connoisseurs? The high culture of Germany was no antidote to barbarism; if anything, it enabled evil to be carried out with a good conscience: "We" are the cultured ones, possessors of a long tradition of great poetry rooted in our national history; "they" are rootless cosmopolitans, their "art" is only mimicry, a trick that parrots or monkeys could learn. Let them play our music at Theresienstadt; it will convince others of our decency. But when we are by ourselves, we will purify our culture from infection by these less than men, these subhumans *(Unter-Menschen).*

There is a sense in which Adorno is right. We cannot hear Beethoven or read Hegel in a naive or straightforward way again. Not to mention Wagner or Heidegger. Even Nietzsche must be seen through the double perspective of what was made of him as well as what he would have made of himself.

And yet. And yet Adorno himself never ceased to look for the art that could transcend the limitations of art, to find the anti-art that could introduce a moment of negativity into the affirmative essence of culture. Similarly Nietsche renounced Wagner only in order to create a new myth: the eternal return and the coming of the Overman *(Ubermensch)*. Zarathustra's story is about the value of stories for life; still, it remains a story; i.e., it stays within the domain of art. And when, at the end of his sanity, Nietzsche identifies himself as both Dionysus and "the crucified", we see that the myth of the will to power is necessary precisely because existence weighs upon us as infinite suffering.

Does this lead us back to the notion of a tragic wisdom? Perhaps. However, Terence Des Pres, in his book, *The Survivor: An Anatomy of Life in the Death Camps,* argues that the phenomenon of the death camps shows that the era of the tragic hero is over:

> If by heroism we mean the dramatic defiance of superior individuals, then the age of heroes is gone. If we have in mind glory and grand gesture, the survivor is not a hero. He or she is anyone who manages to stay alive in body *and* in spirit, enduring dread and hopelessness without the loss of will to carry on in human ways.[9]

In this sense, Juliek is a hero; Wiesel, a survivor.

The survivor chooses to live. "The ordeal of survival becomes, at least for some, an experience of growth and purification...Their will to survive is one with the thrust of life itself, a strength beyond hope".[10] Des Pres equates this strength with "the power of life in itself", a fundamental bodily will to live.

The psychologist Robert Jay Lifton has elaborated this theme of the survivor into a theory of symbolization and art. For Lifton, the survivor is primarily a creator. Survival depends upon his or her ability to imagine extremity, to give it artistic form. Art is not a luxury which we indulge in after our basic survival needs are met. Rather, in an age of mass destruction, only the capacity to imagine our fate can equip us to survive. "If one is to overcome psychic numbing, one must break out from the illusions supporting that numbing and begin to 'imagine the real'".[11]

Art is thus a vital necessity. What Auschwitz has taught us, in fact, is that art is necessary for life. There must be poetry after Auschwitz, if we are to survive. And particularly the poetry which depicts mass destruction, which looks into the abyss and "shows" it to us in all its horror. If art was ever "affirmative", it can no longer be so. The "imagery of extinction" is necessary to enable us to go on living and to make life possible for future generations.

It is interesting that for Lifton, the work of Samuel Beckett best exemplifies the literature of survival. Beckett's characters are without illusion; they live in a world in which the symbolic connection to the tradition of past and future generations is broken. They have no reason to hope or to go on living. And yet. And yet, in the last words of the anonymous narrator of *The Unnameable,* "...I can't go on. I'll go on". They continue. And in this continuation we see the power of life itself when all *"Schein"* is gone. Beckett is able to imagine extremity and in so doing to symbolically reveal a world without symbols, an anti-aesthetic reality. Beckett's plays and novels thus provide an objective correlative for the despair of the survivor. Yet they are not themselves in any way grim; playful, absurd, they celebrate mere existence, just going on. Paradoxically, Beckett's art presents a world without art, without culture. But it is just in "showing" us this world that we are able to accept its truth without despair.

Perhaps this is the point at which we can return to our earlier question: What does Adorno's perspective have to tell us about expressive therapy, viz., about the therapeutic power of art? The first thing that is evident is that art cannot be therapeutic if it aestheticizes suffering, if it distances us from our pain and makes it pleasing or pleasurable. Art, if it is to heal, cannot be a defense against suffering.

Rather, what the sufferer must do is find a way to contain his or her pain just as it is, in all its "ugliness" or "chaos". Thus there must be a struggle against the traditional canons of high culture; therapeutic art knows only one value: to show the truth as far as that is possible. When beauty comes, if it does, it will come out of that truth, not as a veil drawn over it.

From this point of view, the role of the expressive therapist also becomes clear. The therapist is not there to provide reassurance or to give hope. There is nothing to hope for, nothing to hold on to; the therapist must be able to descend into that nothingness without holding on even to "therapy" or "art". It is a matter of survival: When all illusions are gone, what is there to live for? The therapist is the one who is willing to ask that question with the client, to be there while the other struggles to answer it, to witness this struggle and to receive the words and images that express it.

Is this love? If so, it is certainly a hard kind of love, a love without comfort but perhaps deeper for that. This is the love that Is this love? If so, it is certainly a hard kind of love, a love without comfort but perhaps deeper for that. This is the love that is willing to go into the abyss, that can witness the burning of the self and yet hope against hope that new life will emerge.

Healing after Auschwitz means survival. Expressive therapy teaches the art of survival, survival through the making of art. Why art? Because nothing else is strong enough to contain the destruction of the self. Not art as entertainment or art as high culture or art as kitsch, but art as the form of infinite suffering.

And again, as in Beckett, such art need not be sad or grim. The clown can hold my pain as well as the tragic hero; perhaps the clown *is* the hero with a red nose on. Gallows humour? Perhaps. But there is laughter which comes from acknowledging the truth in all its nakedness. Even in the camps, as Frankl reminds us, "Humour was another of the soul's weapons in the fight for self-preservation."[12] The image of extremity is also the image of the absurd.

After Auschwitz we cannot go on as before. And yet we must go on. With art. Without illusion. With the faith that comes when everything has been taken away. With the will to live and to live with others. Only if we can "imagine the real" will we be able to make a life worth living. The therapeutic power of art lies in its capacity to render life valuable by showing both its horror and its pity. If we hold fast to this task, we may be blessed with the presence of joy.

References

1. Appelfeld, Aharon, in Lewis, Stephen ed., *Art Out of Agony: The Holocaust Theme in Literature, Sculpture and Film,* Toronto, 1984, p. 16.

2. Wiesel, Elie, in Lewis, op. cit., p. 167.

3. Friedlander, Saul, *Reflections of Nazism,* New York, 1986, pp. 54-55.

4. Wiesel, in Lewis, op. cit., p. 155.

5. Wiesel, *Night/Dawn/Day,* New York, 1985, p. 119.

6. Wiesel, in Lewis, op. cit., p. 166.

7. Wiesel, *Night/Dawn/Day,* pp. 100-101.

8. Wiesel, in Lewis, op. cit., p. 160.

9. Des Pres, Terence, *The Survivor: An Anatomy of Life in the Death Camps,* New York, 1977. p. 5.

10. Ibid., pp. 21-22.

11. Lifton, Robert Jay, "The Survivor as Creator", in *The Future of Immortality and Other Essays for a Nuclear Age,* New York, 1987, pp. 255-256.

12. Frankl, Viktor E., *Man's Search for Meaning: An Introduction to Logotherapy,* New York, 1966, p. 68.

Once More Into the Ovens

(for P.K., who saw his childhood friend taken away)

Who would have thought I'd find the eye of God
looking up at me from the back of a butterfly
at the foot of my driveway in Chilmark,
not accusingly for a change
but with the calm assurance of the dead?

If God is dead, that doesn't mean
he stops watching us,
only that he ceases to punish
and to judge.
Everything is permitted;
no one cares.

The eye is Horus,
come back to taunt the Jews:
"What about *my* first born, assholes?
All you can think of is,
'The Pyramids and the Jewish Question'.
You're just a chapter in our illustrated book,
papyrus like butterflies
etched in orange and gold."

What's the difference?
We're all brothers under the skin,
colonized creatures, incapable of flight.
God sees the truth but waits,
as time flies into the wind.
A dead bug, its eye watching
our little lives run down.

Something persists, but I don't know its name,
and I don't think it loves us.
Indifferent, watchful, out of time,
it waits for us to see:

"I am God watching God.
I am Pharoah, Moses, Miriam,
the sea that swallows all.
I am the eye on the back of a butterfly
looking up at you from the foot
of your driveway in Chilmark.
Go and sin no more.
Do justice, love mercy
and walk humbly with your God.
If he is dead,
carry his body to your bed
and lie there with him,
watching him breathe.
When the dead awake,
their wings will be restored.
They will fly up, winking,
a panoply of orange and gold.
Believe this and you are saved.
I'm watching you and I can wait.
Can you?
Can you see?
Can you see at last?"

Like smoke from the chimneys,
these words rise up to sing.
Praise, lament, what does it matter?
It's all over now.
Beyond good and evil,
we all suffered in the end.

Let something last, oh,
let something last.

The ashes mingle and re-form.
Not just spirit, our bodies come too,
the thereness of them -
this, here, now,
a moment, monument, majestic sight -
the eye of God -
and I have seen his face and lived
to tell you all.

Written in the day of our Lord, June 18, 1991, C.E., in the
town of Chilmark, island of Martha's Vineyard, country of
America, planet Earth, galaxy one among trillions.

May the martyrs' souls rise up in flight
and soar above this world of pain.
Amen.

BROOKLYN MEMORIES

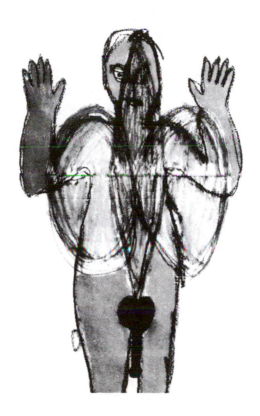

Brooklyn Memories

When I was a kid in Brooklyn,
my friends used to call me "hairy asshole".
I felt ashamed and wondered if it were true.
Was I so abnormal, so hirsute,
so bushy in the tail?
I had another friend
we all called "crud balls".
Now where did that come from?

I guess it was all a kind of affection,
the only kind boys know.

This morning I was lying in bed
feeling the hair between my legs.
It's true! I *am* a hairy asshole,
though no one knows my real name.

I wish we could be boys together again,
playing in the schoolyard,
singing "Ming the Merciless"
and teasing the little kids.
I remember Bobby Levy beat me up once.
I felt totally helpless when
he linked his arms under my legs
and lifted me off the ground.
I kept saying, "I'm not afraid of you",
like a mantra to purify my soul.
It's the same thing Robert Mann said to me
when we got into a fight a while later.
We used to look at the girl's sweaters.
Naomi Schiff wore cashmere,

she had a big bust that seemed so soft.
And we'd wrestle Judy Lipschitz to the ground
just to cop a quick feel.
Who was the girl who dared me
to touch her breasts in class?
I offered to meet her after school
but she just laughed.

I was so tall in the eighth grade
the principal called me, "Big Fella".
Talk about assholes!

Norman Mailer went to the same school
in Brooklyn that I did,
P.S. 161.

It's all gone now, that world.
Blacks and Hasidic Jews replaced us secular yids,
all-Americans in love with rock'n roll.

Forty years later I sit in Toronto,
dreaming a clown show
called, "Fools for Love".
The only men who have friends are gay
and they're all dying.
I still get crushes on girls.
Three different women told me last week
that the beauty I see in others is my own.

It's easier to see myself
the way my friends did.

If only we'd known we were all beautiful!
If only we'd loved each other straight!

The face of Allen Ginsberg
looks up at me from the jacket cover
of his biography.
Now there's a hairy asshole
and proud of it!

Allen, I wish you were my brother
and could teach me how to cross
the street of dreams,
imagination's mysteries.
You were a Jewish kid like me once.
I salute your courage to love.

My youngest son was Bar Mitzvah'd last month.
In a tiny French restaurant,
we careened to the sounds of the
Flying Bulgar Klezmar band,
a blast from the past.

Allen, I wish you were there
to give us your blessing.

Sitting on the toilet writing this poem,
I'm invoking your spirit.

All things are holy!
Hairy assholes are holy!
Brooklyn memories are holy!
Poets bless!

Bless me, Allen, let me be
a son of the commandment,
a son of Orpheus, of Blake,
of Whitman, of Hopkins,
of you.

Bless my memories with these words.
Bless all Brooklyn children.
Bless the bag lady on Bloor Street in Toronto.
Bless Saddam Hussein and George Bush!
Bless the dead,
particularly the dead.

When we rise again, we'll be
exactly as we were.
No transformation.
No purification.
I'll still be a fool for love,
still be a hairy asshole,
still be beautiful if I only
knew how to see myself.

I love you, Allen.
You gave me *Howl* in 1958,
when I thought only I
was crazy in white America.
You gave me *Kaddish* for Naomi
to bless my own mother's madness.
You gave me *Wichita Vortex Sutra*,
when I was off in cloud cukoo-land,
hating the earth.

You gave me this poem.

Something holy abides.
Something holy abides.
Something holy abides.

Bless the child I am.
Bless the child I am.
Bless the child I am.

Mother

Mother, you were larger than life,
stranger than fiction,
a parody of a cliché:
the Jewish Mother in all her glory:
"Eat! Eat! You must be hungry."

I guess I am.

So many lambchops.
And the chocolate cake from Ebinger's.
Later, Leonard's cheesecake
became the holy wafer
that you served for the communion meal.
And the lox! And the cream cheese!
Bagels with eyes wide open!
White fish! Sturgeon!
All the emblems of your majesty.

I remember the postcard of an enormous steak
you sent us when you feared we might die
of vegetable overdose,
and the meals at the Assembly
where my father encouraged me
to order the choicest cuts.

Eat! Eat!
It's a wonder I'm not anorexic.
Everything going into my mouth, ingesting.
You entered me through my mouth,
as you did through my anus
in the days of enemas and purges.

Mother, did you know you were intrusive?
Were you afraid I would leave
if you didn't go inside me?

I am filled with you, stuffed.
You clog up my orifices,
stop my mouth, my cock, my ass.
I am a mummy
wrapped with your concern.

Truly the past lives on!
Truly we are what others
have put inside us!

Without you I am empty,
waiting, longing to be fed.

Come back, Mother!
You will sit at our table,
flesh rotting, stench of decay,
passing around the coffee cake,
urging us on.
"Eat! Eat!",
your grave voice will shriek.

And I will be happy
in my familiarity with you.
Content to consume your flesh,
suck your bones and
feast on your heart.

I take you in entirely.
Flesh of my flesh, bone of my bone.
I have eaten you,
and I have won.

Father

Now I understand Kierkegaard
better than he understood himself,
waiting for Regina in the cold dawn
of an eternal silence.
What was his sin?
To curse his father's name?
Many of us have done worse
or better.

Isaac brooding day after day,
"What if He hadn't changed His mind?
What would you have done then?"

My father, mute, inarticulate,
wanting only the best for me,
vanishing so as not to get in my way.
Must I curse him?

Even when with compassion I trace your footsteps back to
that small village in Poland/Russia, the six-year old traveling
to the *goldene medinah*, mother dying, new wife an archetypal step-mother, working in Uncle's grocery store, protect-
ing younger brother, surviving in the promised land, buying
the American dream, and your children grown, ungrateful,
destroyed, foreign to you, no war, no catastrophe, just day
after day where no harm happens, nor much else, clipping
coupons, shopping at the A & P, reading junk novels, the
Times, the *Journal,* and your son, the poet, civil disobediant,
alien, contemptuous or not, but rejecting all of it, except

the money, money which protects, feeds, charms and keeps your wife in a frenzy of spending, saving, giving, not giving, planning, witholding, "Do you think we're made of money?", yes, sadly, I do, and you holding the line, conserving, successful, respected, an honest man, trustee at the Temple, gives to the blind, never niggardly with your youngest son, what more can you do? what else is there? yes, even when with compassion, I re-trace the curved journey of your life, even when I re-collect your softness in age, the way I finally understood your silence not as indifference but as an inability to be loved, even then I do not know if I can bless you, can accept my own sacrificial life.

Father, you denied me my manhood.
There was something missing in you
which I am still searching for,
something the goyim use to murder with,
a wildness, power, masculine grace.
Perhaps you wanted to spare me this,
perhaps you gave me the only protection you knew.
But now I sit in Chilmark,
wondering about my roots,
wanting to find the strength of ancestry.
I need the patriarch that you denied,
need him to measure myself against,
to confront, to conquer or be slain.

This is a terrible testimony -
in these times when manhood is maligned
or made into myth,
I just wish you had more balls,
and that's the truth.
Even with compassion and understanding,
I wish this.

And now I feel a blessing coming on,
some sadness, wisdom,
acceptance of my fate.

Oh father, I bless your gentle ways,
your sweetness which I too share,
your will to do no harm,
your goodness and your piety.
Bless me for all my sins,
my waywardness, unfaithfulness,
my fear and my despair.
Truly I am your son,
do not deny me.
Even as I grew away from you,
there was a bond.
I forgive you for what you could not do.
Grant me the strength to forgive myself.
Bless me, father, though I am
unworthy of your goodness.
Bless the life in me, the love,
the willingness to reach out into the world,
my laughter, joy, my sex,
my wound and my power to heal,
my fathering of sons, my marriage.
Bless me, father, for I have sinned,
I fall down and am unable to rise,
I cry out and the pain
leads me back to you.

This is your last will and testament,
my patrimony, worth more than
all the stocks and bonds,
a gift from God knows where,
but I accept it, accept you,
accept myself as best I can.

A blessing always in this pain,
a healing in my sorrow.
Now I can stand, have fathered myself,
made morning absolution, confession,
the poem my only means of penance.

Where will it end?
In Reagan's legacy to white America?
Where will my children go?
I can only wish them well.
Be brave, boys.
Curse and bless me as you will.
I leave you my willingness to love.
I will not sacrifice you
by holding back my heart.
I give you all my power and my pain,
my weakness and my strength.
Find your own way. Your will. Your art.
Make your lives in struggle and in joy.
Many times have I failed you
and many times have I held you in my arms.
My blessing, passed down from generations,
do not cease fighting me
until you have it.

I am a man.
I am cut and bleeding.
I am healed.
I curse and bless.
I offer you myself.
I am a man.

A Prayer

Could have been a Hasid,
could have worn beard and side-locks,
black coat and hat, hands behind my back,
bent over, smelling of gefilte fish and yiddishkeit,
could have prayed all day and had seven kids,
followed the rebbe wherever he went,
could have been holy.
But doubting mind held me back,
yearning heart held me back,
aching loins held me back,
not enough faith, not enough trust.

So when I read the *Hasidic Tales of the Holocaust*
and marvel at the steady light of piety
illuminating the abyss, I know
that were I to be poised on its lip,
I would have no one to call on
except a God who does not intervene in man's affairs,
who waits for me to visit him,
who is finally incommensurable, unnameable
and absent from scenes of mass destruction.

And I wish it were different,
wish I belonged to a greater community,
wish I had a rebbe/father to guide my steps,
wish my prayers were answered.
But instead I sit here in Chilmark
guilty as ever, lonely as ever,

remembering childhood days on Crown Street,
when the old men walked by, covered in black,
backs bent, hands clasped behind,
and it is as if I were looking into
another universe, frozen in time,
and I know I can never be part of it,
never be anything but what I am:
secular Jew, urban Yid,
friend of Kafka, Rilke, Beckett,
lone survivor of centuries of faith,
displaced person, alien in America,
alien in Judea, homeless, alone.

What keeps me from suicide?
Where is my faith?
Children, marriage, friends, students -
none of these enough.
When I lose all hope, then I know
there is something waiting for me,
a God of extremity,
God in the abyss, not outside of it.
As if I have to give up everything
before I can find Him, as if
my piety grows out of my despair.

Is this what being a Hasid means?
Am I pious in spite of all I am?
I sit here writing,
my beard and sidelocks flowing,
black coat and hat, head nodding,
ready to walk down the road,
bent over, hands behind my back.

5223

O Lord of last resorts,
You teach me not to put trust in
things of the world, You teach me
that I am unable to stand alone.
Let me come back a pious man,
let me observe the Law in all I do,
the dharma of attachment and release.

I leap into the flames,
my coat ablaze,
reciting the *Shema*,
believing in You.